BIBLE
INF●GRAPHICS
FOR KIDS

ACTIVITY BOOK

HARVEST
kids

HARVEST HOUSE PUBLISHERS
Eugene, Oregon

CREATED BY

HARVEST HOUSE BIBLE INFOGRAPHICS TEAM

Brian Hurst	Heather Green	Aaron Dillon	Kyle Hatfield	Nicole Dougherty	Kyler Dougherty
ILLUSTRATOR EXTRAORDINARE	CRAZE-MAZING GENERATOR	MASTER WORDSMITH	GENIUS MAZE CREATOR	CREATIVE BOOK COVER AND INTERIOR DESIGNER NINJAS	

MEET THE REST OF THE CREW

DONKEY
Official Unofficial Mascot and Activity Book Guide. A bit of a sassy pants.

UNICORN
One of a kind, loves the King James translation. A real party animal.

GIRAFFE
Always sticking neck out to assist others. (Recently left career in the toy industry.)

HIPPO
Likes to be large and in charge, but disappears for most of the book. Somewhat hippo-critical.

LION
Mane complainer. Has got quite an appetite.

BEAR
States the obvious, sometimes unbearably.

Bible Infographics for Kids Activity Book
Published by Harvest House Publishers
Eugene, Oregon 97408
www.harvesthousepublishers.com
ISBN 978-0-7369-8222-1 (pbk.)

Printed in China

20 21 22 23 24 25 26 27 28 / RDS / 10 9 8 7 6 5 4 3 2 1

"It's impossible to make *Bible Infographics for Kids* any better."

—Everyone

WELL, CHALLENGE ACCEPTED!

Because now YOU get to experience Bible infographics in the most craze-mazingly creative way yet.

It can't possibly get more craze-mazing— we checked.

Prepare (if you can) to solve perplexing puzzles and masterfully crafted mazes, translate Bible verses into emojis, muster up some ad-lib stories, craft new creations, doodle, write, search, find, experiment...plus a lot more!

"More?" you ask in total shock.

Well, we didn't want to crazily un-craze the craze-mazing content contained between covers.

Seriously... spoilers?

It doesn't matter where you start, just that you do. An incredible experience—where the Bible comes to life in a whole new way—is waiting!

So why are you still here?

You should go.

You're *still* reading the introduction?

Do you not like fun?

Of course you do.

GO!

That means turn the page, silly.

GOD'S EPICALLY AWESOME BOOK

The Bible is made up of **66 DIFFERENT BOOKS** written by **MORE THAN 40 AUTHORS!**

How many books do you have?

Count the number of books you can find in your room: **95**

Keep going and count all the books in your house: **300**

The Bible is the bestselling book of all time, ever (by far)—It's sold more than 5 billion copies! Wow!

Let's do some math!

An average book is 7" tall. Multiply the number of books you counted in your whole house and multiply that by 7. That will tell you how far your books will stretch.

300 x 7" = **2,100** ÷ 12" = _____

| number of books in your house | how many inches your books will stretch | how many feet your books will stretch |

Will they stretch out your room? Down the hallway? Across the yard? Out of state?

The Bible was written over a span of 1,500 years (remember, by 40 different people). Wow!

What is the oldest book you could find?

Oliver Twist

What's your favorite book?

Minecraft

Check on the inside of the book for the copyright page. Some tiny-tiny number will be hiding in there telling you what year it was printed.

Draw your own Bible cover!

IT'S ALL **GREEK** TO ME!

The New Testament was mostly written in Koine Greek. It originally had no punctuation and no spaces between words, and it was all capitalized. Must have been pretty hard to read!

THENEWTESTAMENTWASORIGINALLYWRITTENLIKETHISWITHNOSPACESBETWEENWORDSITHADNOPUNCTUATIONANDNOPARAGRAPHBREAKSITWASWRITTENWITHNOVERSENUMBERSCHAPTERNUMBERSORSECTIONHEADINGSTHESEWEREADDEDLATERTOHELPREADERSLIKEYOU

Can you figure out these messages written in the same way?

1 INTHEBEGINNINGGODCREATEDTHEHEAVENSANDTHEEARTH

2 FORGODSOLOVEDTHEWORLDTHATHEGAVEHISONEANDONLYSONTHATWHOEVERBELIEVESINHIMSHALLNOTPERISHBUTHAVEETERNALLIFE

3 THENEWTESTAMENTALSOWASWRITTENWITHOUTVERSENUMBERSCHAPTERNUMBERSORSECTIONHEADINGSTHESEWEREADDEDLATERTOHELPREADERSLIKEYOU

4 WHATSYOURFAVORITEFLAVOROFICECREAMWRITEOUTTHEANSWERBELOW

Turn to page 118 to find the answer key.

THE EMOJI STANDARD TRANSLATION (EST)

The Bible has not only been sold more than any other book, ever, it's also been translated into many more languages than any other book...even emoji!

Translate some of your favorite verses into Emoji.

Here's an example.

"The joy of the LORD is your strength." Nehemiah 8:10

EMOJI TRANSLATION:

Your turn! Try translating this verse.

"The heavens declare the glory of God." Psalm 19:1

EMOJI TRANSLATION:

My favorite verse:

EMOJI TRANSLATION:

Here are some example emojis to inspire you:

THE STORY OF CREATION

The paraphrased story of creation on the next page is missing a few details. To discover the full story... FIRST fill in the blanks below without peeking at the story. THEN copy the words you wrote beside each number into the story on the next page.

1. GameStop — place
2. Walmart — place
3. great — adjective
4. perfect — adjective
5. Asher — person
6. fork — noun
7. spoon — noun
8. spork — noun
9. book — noun

10. street — noun
11. bacon — type of food
12. sporks — noun, plural
13. napkin — noun
14. plate — noun
15. Kraken — type of sea creature
16. airplane — thing that flies
17. sporks — noun, plural
18. weird — adjective
19. mad — adjective
20. jump — command
21. smart — adjective

A **noun** is a person, place, or a thing (such as teacher, book, or street), and an **adjective** describes a noun (such as clean, jolly, little, or blue).

Don't worry if it doesn't sound right—you can read the real story in Genesis 1:1–2:4.

8

In the beginning God created 1. *Gamestop* and 2. *Walmart*

DAY 1 – The earth was 3. *great* and 4. *perfect*. There was darkness, and 5. *Asher* was hovering over the surface. God separated the light from the darkness, and called the light " 6. *Tonk* " and the darkness " 7. *spoon* ."

DAY 2 – God separated the waters above from the waters below and called the in-between space " 8. *Sponk* ."

DAY 3 – God separated the waters from dry ground. He named them " 9. *book* " and " 10. *Street* ." Then, 9. *book* produced 11. *bacon* . And God saw that it was good.

DAY 4 – God separated the day from the night. He created 12. *Sporks*, 13. *napkin* to govern the day, and 14. *plate* to govern the night. And God saw that it was good.

DAY 5 – God filled the seas with 15. *Kraken* , and created 16. *airplane* to fill the sky. And God saw that it was good.

DAY 6 – Then God said, "Let us make 17. *Sporks* in our image." So God created 17. *sponks* ; 18. *weird* and 19. *mad* he created them. God blessed them and said to them, " 20. *jump* ." God saw all that he had made, and it was very good.

Thus 1. *Gamestop* and 2. *Walmart* were completed.

DAY 7 – God had finished the work he had been doing; so on the seventh day he rested from all his work. Then God blessed the seventh day and made it 21. *smart* .

...zZZ

9

GOD'S CREATION

Connect the dots to find out what God created on day two of creation.

When you're all done, add your own details or color it in!

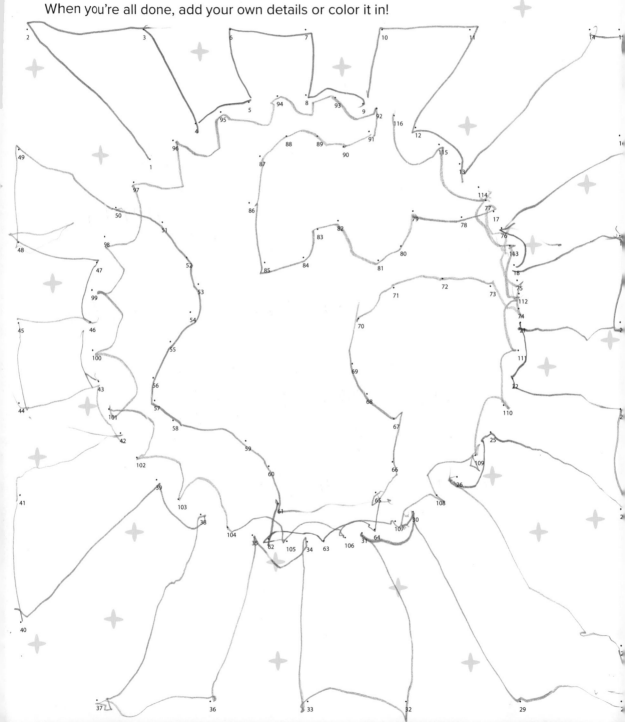

SEA AND SKY—SPOT WHAT DOESN'T BELONG!

God created the sky and the sea to be filled with living creatures! Take a close look at this picture and spot what doesn't belong.

There are **46 objects** that don't belong in the sky or the sea. See if you can find them all! Turn to page 126 to find the answer key.

WHERE ON EARTH DID IT ALL BEGIN?

God did AMAZING things when He created the entire universe out of nothing! Use the clues to figure out which galactic words fill in the blanks.

When you're all done, the yellow column will form a hidden message!

Clues:

1   a system of millions or billions of stars

2   moves in orbit around a planet

3   what Adam was made out of

4   when the moon crosses between the earth and the sun, or the earth crosses between the moon and the sun

5   a fixed bright point in the night sky

6   the most basic form of a material, like what's found in the periodic table

7   a day of rest

8   the distance that light travels in one year

9   a distinctive pattern of stars in the night sky

10   a small rocky body orbiting the sun

11   the galaxy that contains the earth (or an amazing candy bar)

12   lasting or existing forever, without end or beginning

13   it moves in orbit around a star

14   a concentration of mass so dense that nothing can escape its gravitational pull

15   a group of planets revolving around a sun

1. galaxy
2. moon
3. dust
4. ellipse
5. star
6. element
7. sabbath
8. light-year
9. constellation
10. asteriod
11. Milky way
12. eternal
13. planet
14. black hole
15. Solar system

Turn to page 120 to find the answer key.

Hidden Message:

God created it all

Let's imagine that Noah and his three sons, Shem, Ham, and Japheth, each took care of one of the four levels of the ark. Each level contained different types of **animals**: wild animals, livestock, animals that live on the ground, and birds.

Look at the clues below to figure out **where** each animal lived, **who** cared for that level, and **what day** that animal checked on the rainfall.

R Roof Deck

U Upper Deck

M Middle Deck

L Lower Deck

Clues

1. Halfway through the rainfall, this animal reached its long neck up through the skylight and it felt the rain still falling.

2. Japheth brought some rainwater all the way to the middle deck to create mud for the pig to roll around in.

3. Noah kept the snakes as far away as possible from the birds.

4. On the last day of rain, Ham released the dove, who saw that the rain was stopping.

5. This animal slithered all the way up to the top level on the thirtieth day to see if the rain was still falling.

Use this chart to keep track of the clues where the boxes intersect. Mark an X where you know there's a wrong answer, and a √ where you know there's a right answer. Turn to page 123 to find the solution.

	Giraffe	Pig	Snake	Dove
R Roof Deck				√
U Upper Deck	√			
M Middle Deck		√		
L Lower Deck			√	
Noah			√	
Shem	√			
Ham				√
Japheth		√		
10 Day 10		√		
20 Day 20	√			
30 Day 30			√	
40 Day 40			√	

DOODLE CREATION

Close your eyes and draw a random doodle on the page below.

It can loop, zigzag, swirl, or crisscross.

Now, take a step back and, just like finding animal shapes in clouds, see what kind of creatures you can imagine in your squiggles. Add in more detail and color, and name your new creations!

Bird

MIX-AND-MATCH CREATURES

Use the animals listed here as inspiration and mix-and-match parts of them to create your very own unique animal creations!

Then, like Adam, give each of them a name!

lion	rhino	eagle	moose	rabbit	stingray	swan
elephant	monkey	frog	ostrich	octopus	shark	starfish
penguin	bat	hippo	owl	raccoon	pig	crab
horse	snake	hummingbird	mouse	sheep	chicken	crocodile
zebra	camel	panda	peacock	squirrel	llama	dolphin

Example: The ears of a _____, the legs of a _____, and the body of a _____.

N-O-A-H-'S A-R-K

Turn each of these letters into an animal you'd find on Noah's Ark.

NOAH

Extra points if the name of the animal begins with that letter!

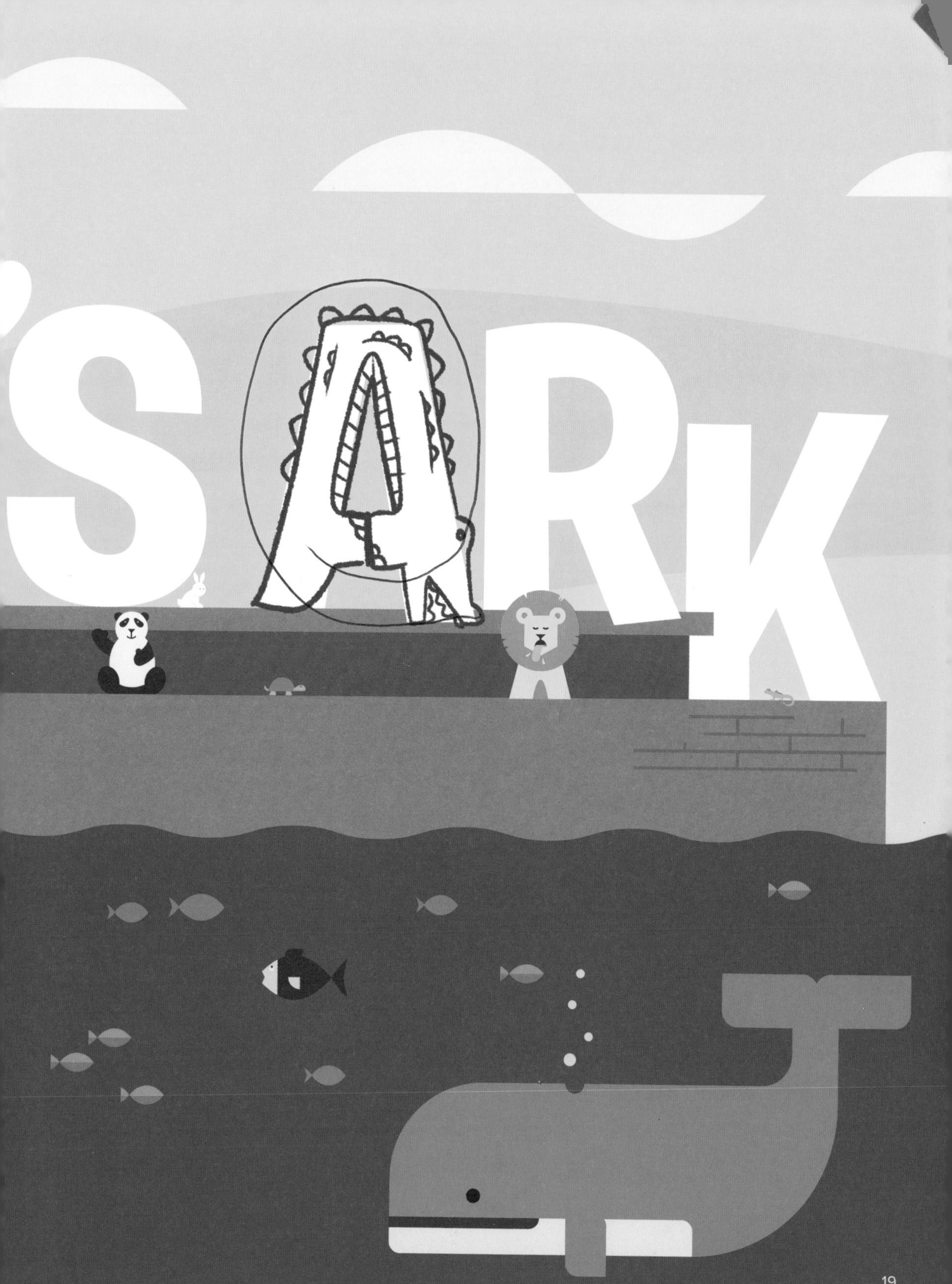
'SARK

DRAW BEHEMOTH

The book of Job mentions a beast called Behemoth.
But we don't know for sure what a Behemoth was.
Was it a mighty mammoth, a water buffalo, or even a hippo?
The Bible doesn't tell us for sure, but it does tell us a little bit:

eats grass like an ox

strong legs

powerful stomach

tail like a cedar tree

bones like bronze

limbs like rods of iron

lives in marshy land

powerful enough to withstand a river

Can you draw a Behemoth that fits this description?
Any guesses what the Bible was referring to?

BEARD ME

Methuselah was the oldest recorded person who ever lived. He lived 969 years!

At some point, he may have gotten a little lost as to what year it was or where he'd come from or where he was going.

Help Methuselah navigate the maze and find his way out!

Turn to page 123 to find the solution.

Methusela celebrated a lot of birthdays. Imagine how many candles he blew out!

Let's do the math...
969 x 970 ÷ 2 = **469,965 candles!**

Wow, that's a lot of candles! Now you try!

10	x	11	=	110
your age		your age + 1		a huge number

110	÷ 2 =	55
same huge number		number of candles

WILL THEY ALL FIT?

The ark was big enough to hold 55,000 species of animals! It would have taken some serious organization to get them all to fit well in the ark.

See if you can help Noah figure out how to fit the animals in the ark.

Turn to pages 129 and 131 and cut out the animal blocks. Figure out how to fit them all into the space perfectly without overlapping or leaving any gaps.

Good luck!

EASY

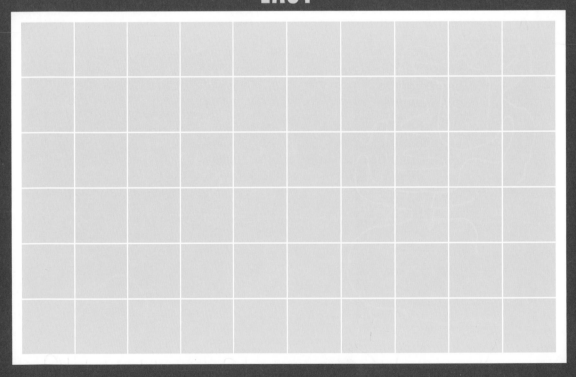

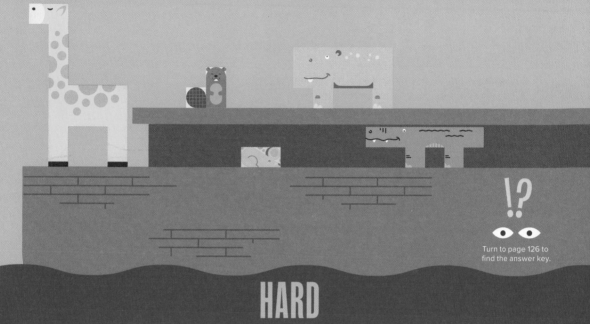

Turn to page 126 to find the answer key.

HARD

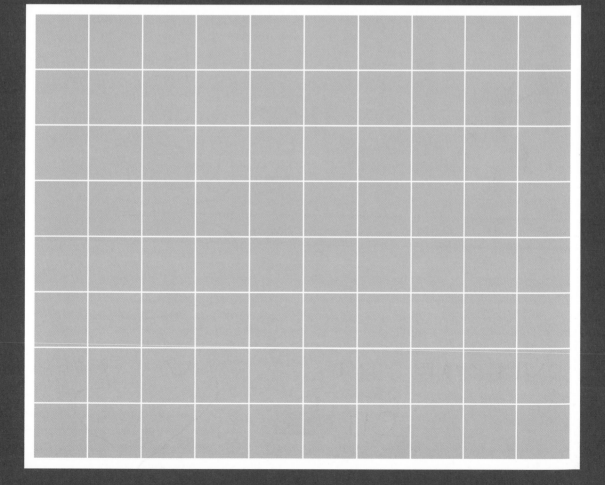

SPOT **LIGHT**

On day 1 of creation, God separated the light from the dark. You're looking at the same scene, but one has light and the other has no light.

Turn to page 125 to find the answer key.

Use your night vision to spot all the differences!

LIGHT AND DARK

Find all the words describing light and dark.

Highlight the "light words" in one color and the "dark words" in another color. When you're all done, the letters that aren't highlighted will make up a secret message!

LIGHT WORDS

LIGHT	STAR
PROTECTION	SUN
GOOD	RAINBOW
ETERNAL	SPECTRUM
COLOR	TRUTH
LIGHT-YEAR	LIFE

DARK WORDS

DARK	INFRARED
FOOLISHNESS	ULTRAVIOLET
EVIL	XRAY
HIDDEN	GAMMARAY
RADIO	BLIND
MICROWAVE	INVISIBLE

```
O N M U R T C E P S D F R
B O R A D I O R I N O A A
M I C R O W A V E O E H I
I T D O O G H B L Y I G N
N C S L I T L I T D X G B
V E H T U I S H D I R Y O
I T N R N H G E E T A R W
S O T D N I N R R R Y O O
I R T E L O I V A R T L U
B P S D A R K M R T S O E
L S L I V E M T F U S C F
E T E R N A L H N E D A I
R K T H G I L N I E S S L
```

Turn to page 122 to find the answer key.

Secret Message:

"G ___ _____

_____ _____

____ _____ !"

To find the secret message, look for unmarked letters. Start in the top left and follow along the rows to the right just like you read a book.

LET'S **MAKE** A **RAINBOW**

Did you know that the light we see is made up of all the colors of the rainbow? We just can't see them all because when the colors are all combined, it looks white! But there are a few ways we can see them. One is in a rainbow.

When light hits water, the light refracts (or separates), forming colors.

R O Y G B I V

Make your own rainbow!

Step 1: Fill a large container halfway with water.

Step 2: Set a mirror in the container, propped up at an angle, so that half of the mirror is underwater and half is above the water.

Step 3: Put the container near a window or under direct light.

Step 4: Hold up a piece of paper or poster board where the light is being reflected so you can see the rainbow!

Be careful not to look directly into the mirror—it will be so bright it will hurt your eyes!

RAINBOWS ARE A-MAZE-ING

Find your way through the rainbow maze!

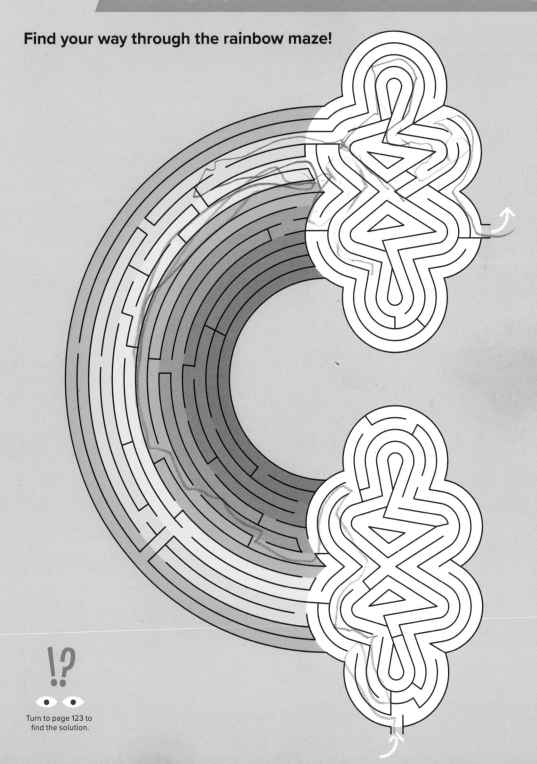

!?

Turn to page 123 to
find the solution.

COLOR BY NUMBER

The colors we see in the world are made up of light. But what if the colors we're used to seeing aren't what they actually are?

Write a different color by each of the numbers below and color the picture by following the number key.

Get creative with it!

1 [ ] 4 [ ]

2 [ ] 5 [ ]

3 [ ] 6 [ ] 7 [ ]

WHAT'S A **LIGHT-YEAR?**

Did you know that it takes years for the light from stars to reach us? It travels at the speed of light (obvi!), so we're actually seeing what the stars looked like in the past!

What are those distant galaxies seeing?

The Alpha Centauri star system is 4.2 light-years away, so the light astronomers see from it is 4.2 years old. **What was happening in your life 4 years and 2 months ago? What was happening in the world then?**

The Sirius star system is 8.6 light-years away, so the light astronomers see from it is 8.6 years old. **What was happening in your life 8 years and 7 months ago?** What was happening in the world then?

The Tau Ceti star system is 11.9 light-years away, so the light astronomers see from it 11.9 years old. **What was happening in your life 11 years and 11 months ago?** What was happening in the world then?

The sun is 93 million miles away, which is .00001581 light-years. So the light we see from it is 8 minutes and 20 second old. **What was happening 8 minutes and 20 seconds ago?**

DID **YOU** SAY **UNICORN?**

The Bible talks about some pretty fantastic animals.
Did you know the unicorn makes an appearance in the King
James Version of the Bible? And not just once, but 9 times!

Create your own fantastic unicorn!

1   Remove and cut out the unicorn origami paper from page 137.

2   With the colored side out,
fold your paper diagonally both ways.

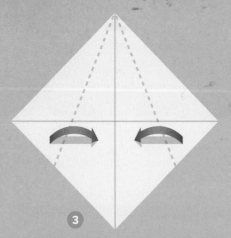 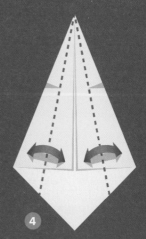

3

Fold the sides in once, making an
upside-down ice cream cone shape.

4

Fold the sides in once again, making
an even skinnier cone! Fold back out.

Yumm, ice cream!

30

5

Fold the top tip down to line up with the bottom tip.

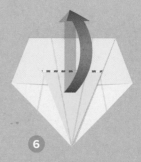

6

Fold the smaller tip back up along the dotted line. This will be the unicorn horn!

Here are the tricky steps!

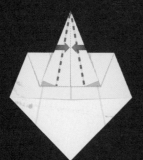

7 Fold the sides of the horn into the center. In order to do this, you'll also need to fold in the sides of the large diamond shape at the same time.

To get all the sides to line up straight in the center, you'll have to make four new little triangles, which are marked by dotted lines on the paper.

8

Use some clear tape to close the back. Flip over, and...

TADA
you have a unicorn!

What word do other versions of the Bible use instead of the unicorn? Check out Numbers 23:22, Psalm 22:21, and Psalm 92:10 in your Bible.

BUILD MOSES BIT BY BIT

An ancient image of Moses has been discovered! Help restore it with this special code.

Blue
A1–A13
A26–A34
B1–B4
B8–B12
B26–B33
C1–C3
C10–11
C31–C32
D1–D2
D11
E1
E10–E11
F30–F34
G31–G34
H30–H34
I1
I10–I11
J1–J2
J11
K1–K3
K10–K11
K31–K32
L1–L4
L8–L12
L26–L33
M1 – M13
M26–M34

Dark Blue
C22–C23
E22–E23
G22–G23
H22–H23
I22–I25
K22–K23

White
C21
C24–C30
D21
D24–D29
E21
E24–E30
F21
F24–F29
G21
G24–G30
H21
H24–H29
I21
I24–I30
J21
J24–J29
K21
K24–K30

Dark Tan
C16–C20
G19
K16–K20

Yellow
D3
D22–D23
E3
E12
F3
F13–F14
F22–F23
G3
G13–G15
H3
H13–H14
I3
I12
J3
J22–J23

Brown
B5–B7
C4–C6
C9
D4–D5
D10
E2
E4
F1–F2
F4
F6
F8
G1–G2
G4
G9
H1–H2
H4
H6
H8
I2
I4
J4–J5
J10
K4–K6
K9
L5–L7

Tan
A14–A25
B13–B25
B34
C7–C8
C12–C15
C33–C34
D6–D9
D12–D20
D30–D34
E5–E9
E13–E20
E31–E34
F5
F7
F9–F12
F15–F20
G5–G8
G10–G12
G16–G18
G20
H5
H7
H9–H12
H15–H20
I5–I9
I13–I20
I31–I34
J6–J9
J12–J20
J30–J34
K7–K8
K12–K15
K33–K34
L13–L25
L34
M14–M25

Follow the color code, and color in the square where the letter and number intersect!

33

THE PLAGUES OF EGYPT

The Bible tells us that God sent 10 plagues to free His people from slavery in Egypt. Help Moses remember the 10 plagues by unscrambling the words below...

Check out Exodus 7–11 for help!

1. LOBOD — *blood*
2. OFSGR — *frogs*
3. SNTAG
4. FLESI
5. LKICOETSV

6. LOSBI
7. LAHI
8. SSUOLCT
9. NDSKSREA
10. TOFIRNSB

Turn to page 118 to find the answer key.

Yikes, these plagues sound terrible. Which plague do you think would be the worst?

flood

What if God had sent an eleventh plague? What would it have been?

Draw your eleventh plague.

Now that Moses can remember the 10 plagues, help the Israelites escape from Pharaoh and the Egyptians.

RED SEA ▶

Turn to page 124 to find the answer key.

THE **FROG** ARMY

In the second plague, the land of Egypt was covered with frogs. Maybe you think frogs are cool, and maybe a plague of frogs wouldn't be too bad. But on the streets, in all the buildings, in every room of your house...can you imagine that?

Let's make an origami frog!

1 Remove and cut out the frog origami paper from page 133.

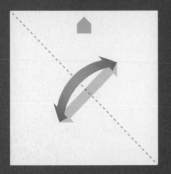

2 Fold your paper along the diagonal. **Unfold.**

3 Fold your paper in half. **Unfold.**

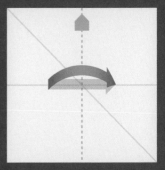

4 Fold in half the other way and leave the paper folded in half.

5 You will see a diagonal across the top half of your paper. Fold along that diagonal. **Unfold.**

6 Repeat the other direction. **Unfold.**

7 You should see an "X" across the top half of the rectangle. Fold down from the top (at the center) to cross through the center of the X. **Unfold.**

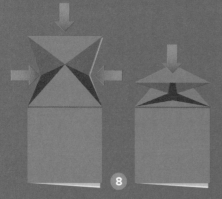

8

Press the sides of the "X" in and fold down.

(You should have a triangle at the top of your paper now.)

9

On the top triangle, fold the outside corners up to the top of the triangle.

(This will form the frog's front legs).

10

Leaving the top section alone, fold the two sides of the bottom rectangle in, meeting in the middle.

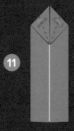

11

On the top section, fold the front legs in half, down, and out.

12

Fold the bottom edge of the rectangle up to the tip of the nose.

13

Fold the bottom edge in half downward.

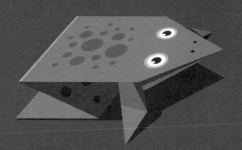

Flip over, and you have
A FROG!

Did you know a group of frogs is called an army? God sent an army of frogs to help free the Israelites!

Bonus:

If you press on the back of the frog, it will jump.

WHOASES, MOSES!

From Egypt to the wild, Moses led a full life. So full, he couldn't keep everything he needed with him.

Find the hidden items below that Moses would have used in the different places he went. And make sure to spot the things we use today—things he surely would have liked to have had on hand!

scroll

map

cup

giraffe

stone tablets

burning bush

comb

serpent

backpack

compass

Promised Land sign

pitchfork

Band-Aid

toothbrush

deodorant

brick of gold

pile of diamonds

tent

ark of the covenant

cupcake

soccer ball

scissors

dice

coins

tombstone

shamrock

ice cube

traveling stick with a bag on the end

RIP

Turn to page 127 to find the answer key.

FAMILY RULES

God has rules for us, but isn't it fun to think of rules for our own family too? To have some fun creating some imaginative rules on your own or with your family, just fill in the blanks below and copy your answers into the list on the next page.

#	Answer	Prompt
1.	Sangatangn	your last name
2.	Kicking	verb ending in -ing
3.	Don't put your hand into a saw	piece of advice
4.	chocolates	kind of food or candy, plural
5.	what is I + I	interesting or fun question
6.	hug	verb
7.	money	noun, plural
8.	kidnappers	type of relative
9.	murder	noun
10.		animal, plural
11.		body part
12.		holiday
13.		day of the week, plural
14.		type of breakfast food
15.		famous or favorite song
16.		cartoon character
17.		verb
18.		famous line from a movie

#	Answer	Prompt
19.		adjective
20.		noun, plural
21.		superhero name
22.		unusual animal, plural
23.		verb ending in -ing
24.		noun, plural
25.		adjective
26.		noun, plural
27.		verb
28.		verb ending in -ed
29.		farm animal, plural
30.		noun, plural
31.		type of clothing
32.		adjective
33.		kind of food
34.		adjective
35.		job or profession, plural
36.		phrase

1. **Smith-Ons** FAMILY RULES

① 2. **Kicking** is mandatory.

② Always tell people 3. **D.P.Y.H.I.A.S.**

③ Have 4. **Chooolates** , ask 5. **1 + 1 = ?** , do not 6. **hug** , and absolutely no 7. **money** !

④ Encourage your 8. **kidnappers** and share in their 9. **mean stuff**

⑤ Obey your 10. **children** .

⑥ Use your 11. **gun** in all circumstances, including 12. **on friends** and 13. **nieces** .

⑦ Too much TV is a bad thing...too much 14. **gaming** is good.

⑧ Sing 15. **Sake it off** dance like 16. **Taylor** , 17. **Swift** often, say " 18. **You shall not pass** " always.

⑨ Be 19. **mean** at all times.

⑩ Keep your 20. **guns** .

-⑪ Always give to 21. **children in** first. **your basements**

⑫ Never leave 22. **home** .

⑬ Share everything, except 23. **cigaretts** + 24. **beer** .

⑭ Don't take 25. **sus** 26. **Yon** that don't belong to you.

⑮ Be happy with the things you 27. **do** and what others 28. **don't** .

⑯ Use nice 29. **cussing** ; ignore bad 30. **speech** . *kind*

⑰ Bless your 31. **Food** , be 32. **rude** , eat 33. **nastily** , clean up after 34. **nobody** 35. ~~~~ .

⑱ Remember to say " 36. **Lawyer** ."

Thank God for this family!

WITH **GOD** ALL THINGS ARE **POSSIBLE!**

Elijah outran a chariot with God's help. A chariot can travel 35 to 40 miles per hour.

Could you outrun a chariot? (No, you couldn't.) But let's see how close you can get!

Ask your parents to drive you to a local track. Time yourself running as fast as you can for ¼ mile (about one lap around the track). Then fill out this worksheet for your answer!

I ran ¼ of a mile in **15** minutes and **20** seconds.

1 **Multiply your minutes by 60.**

315
x 6
90

15 minutes x 60 = **900** seconds

2 **Now add that value to your seconds.**
(This gives you the number of seconds it took you to run ¼ mile.)

67

900 seconds + **20** seconds = **920** seconds

3 **Now multiply your seconds by 4.**
(This gives you the number of seconds it takes to run a mile.)

920 seconds x 4 = **1880** seconds

4 **Divide by 60.**
(This converts back to minutes.)

6) 1,880

1880 seconds ÷ 60 = ____ minutes

5 **Finally, divide 60 by your minutes.**

60 ÷ ____ minutes = ____ mph.

You ran ____ mph —congratulations!

Now draw yourself in the infographic!

Turtle	Name:	Usain Bolt (world's fastest man)	Chariot
4 mph	Speed:	28 mph	35–40 mph

So...are you faster than a turtle?

 Yes   No

God accomplished amazing feats with other people in the Bible too!
Would you rather be like...

Peter

who walked on water

Philip

who teleported 20 miles instantly

Samson

who had superhuman strength and brought down a temple

EPIC BIBLE TRIVIA

Try these challenging trivia questions yourself to see how many you can get right. Or gather up your family, some friends, or your entire church and have a trivia night.

Pizza strongly suggested.

Trivia Rules

1 No cell phones or electronic devices allowed.

2 Decide ahead of time whether Bibles can be used.

3 Remember to have fun! If you don't know an answer, that's okay—make a guess!

PEOPLE IN THE BIBLE

1 **Which person from the Bible had a talking donkey?**

2 **Which person from the Bible lived the longest?**
Bonus point: How long did this person live?

3 **What woman is mentioned most often in the Bible?**

4 **Who was Abraham and Sarah's son?**
Bonus point: What does his name mean?

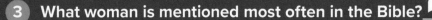

5 **Which person from the Bible didn't die, but was taken up to heaven in a chariot of fire?**

6 **Which person in the Bible was bitten by a snake after being shipwrecked?**

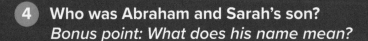

Turn to page 121 to find the answer key.

7 What is the name of the only female judge? *Deborah*

8 Which three people were thrown in a fiery furnace because they wouldn't bow to an idol? *Bonus points for correct spellings!*

 *Meshach, Radghack, and Abendgo*

THE BIBLE

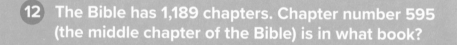

9 How many books are in the Bible?

10 What language was most of the Old Testament written in?

11 What is the tenth book of the Bible?

12 The Bible has 1,189 chapters. Chapter number 595 (the middle chapter of the Bible) is in what book?

13 What is the longest chapter in the Bible?
Bonus point: How many verses does that chapter have?

Psalm 119

14 What is the shortest book of the Bible?

15 Who wrote the most words in the New Testament?

16 What is the second-to-last book of the Bible?

PLACES IN THE BIBLE

17 Jonah was swallowed by a big fish while disobeying God's command to go where?

18 Where was Jesus born? *Bonus point: In what Old Testament book was that location prophesied?*

19 Where did Mary, Joseph, and Jesus escape to after Jesus's birth?

20 Where did Jesus appear to Paul?

21 Which city did Joshua and the Israelites invade by marching around it and blowing on rams' horns?

22 Where did Moses receive the Ten Commandments?

23 Where was the resting place for Noah's Ark?

24 What sea did God part to help the Israelites escape Pharaoh?

POTPOURRI

*That means these are the best-smelling questions...
j/k, it just means a mix of a bunch of things.*

25 What did God make on the sixth day of creation?

26 What was the second Egyptian plague?

27 What three items were inside the Ark of the Covenant?

28 Jesus tells Peter to go fishing and find what
in the mouth of the first fish he caught?

29 Samson used the jawbone of what animal to defeat 1,000 men?

30 What instrument did David play?

31 What gifts did the wise men bring baby Jesus?

32 How many disciples did Jesus choose to travel with Him?
Bonus point: Which of Jesus's disciples was a tax collector?

Turn to page 121 to
find the answer key.

DREAM INTERPRETING

King Nebuchadnezzar had a baffling dream, and no one in his kingdom could interpret it for him. See if you can help!

Choose a word for each of the blanks below and then add them to the story on the next page.

1. _____ adjective

2. _____ verb

3. _____ job/profession

4. _____ job/profession

5. _____ job/profession

6. _____ job/profession

7. _____ quality in a person

8. _____ adjective

9. _____ adjective

10. _____ material or ingredient

11. _____ material or ingredient

12. _____ material or ingredient

13. _____ material or ingredient

14. _____ material or ingredient

15. _____ object, singular

16. _____ adjective

17. _____ noun, singular

18. _____ place

19. _____ adjective

20. _____ adjective

21. _____ verb, past tense

22. _____ verb

God revealed to me what Nebuchadnezzar's dream really meant. You can read about it in Daniel 2!

In the second year of his reign, Nebuchadnezzar had dreams; his mind was

1. _____ and he could not 2. _____ . So the king summoned the

3. _____ , 4. _____ , 5. _____ , and 6. _____

to tell him what he had dreamed...

The king asked Daniel... "Are you able to tell me what I saw in my dream and interpret it?"...

Daniel replied... "This mystery has been revealed to me, not because I have greater

7. _____ than anyone else alive, but so that Your Majesty may know the

interpretation [of your dream].

"There before you stood...an 8. _____ , 9. _____ statue...

The head of the statue was made of pure 10. _____ , its chest and arms of

11. _____ , its belly and thighs of 12. _____ , its legs of

13. _____ , its feet partly of 13. _____ and partly of baked

14. _____ . A 15. _____ ...struck the statue on its feet...and

smashed [the statue to pieces]... The wind swept them away without leaving a trace.

But the 15. _____ that struck the statue became a 16. _____

17. _____ and filled the whole 18. _____ .

"This was the dream, and now we will interpret it to the king... You are that head of

10. _____ .

"After you, another kingdom will arise, inferior to yours. Next, a third kingdom, one of

12. _____ , will rule over the whole 18. _____ . Finally, there will be

a fourth kingdom, strong as 13. _____ ...so it will crush and break all the

others... The feet and toes were partly of baked 14. _____ and partly of

13. _____ , so this will be a divided kingdom... This kingdom will be partly

19. _____ and partly 20. _____ ...

"The God of heaven will set up a kingdom that will never be 21. _____ ...

It will 22. _____ all those kingdoms and bring them to an end, but it will itself

endure forever."

DREAM DIARY

God gave Daniel the ability to interpret certain dreams that told about the future.

Our dreams may not be caused by anything more than the pizza we had for dinner, but it's still fun to think about our dreams.

In this dream diary, write down or draw the dreams you have this week.

...zzZ

FAMILY LAWS—GUIDELINES REALLY

God gives us some pretty important rules and laws to follow!

From the Ten Commandments (Exodus 20:1-17) to the Golden Rule (Matthew 7:12) to the greatest commandment (Matthew 22:36-40), it seems like a good idea to have some guidelines in our lives.

So, what about some family rules? When everyone is on the same page, everyone benefits and it can help us follow God's instructions.

What rules can you and your family come up with below?

I. Put God first.

II. Love Jesus and each other.

III. Be silly.

IV. Always share pizza.

V. Don't wake Mom when she's napping.

MAKE A JERICHO HORN

God told the Israelites to march around the walled city of Jericho once a day for 6 days. On the seventh day, they were to march around it 7 times, and the priests were to blow their horns, and the walls would come tumbling down. What a crazy way to win a battle!

The horns used in that day were called shofars, and they were typically made from ram horns.

Let's make your own shofar!

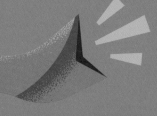

Supplies

2 sheets of paper *(preferably something thick, like card stock or construction paper)*
tape
things to decorate with *(markers, crayons, stickers, glitter, etc.)*

Instructions

1 Roll one of the sheets of paper lengthwise into a cone shape. Use a few pieces of tape to keep the paper in its cone shape.

2 Roll the second sheet of paper into a tube. Tape it together.
IMPORTANT: The tube should be just wide enough to fit over the wide part of the cone.

3 Place the tube over the wide part of the cone and then tilt it at an angle to imitate a ram's horn. Tape the two pieces of paper together.

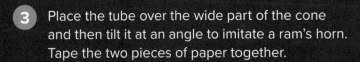

Shofar, sho good!

4 Decorate your horn however you like. Feel free to go crazy!

5 Blow your horn!

BATTLE OF THE BOXES

The Bible is full of battles, and a big part of that was over the land or territory. Find out if you can beat your friends at this game!

1 Play rock, paper, scissors to see who will go first.

2 Each player must take a turn connecting two dots together, either up and down or side to side (no diagonals).

3 If you complete a box, put your first initial or a shape to show that that is one of your boxes!

4 For every box you complete you also get a free turn. Whoever makes the most boxes wins!

DONKEY DECODER

Remember that time Balaam's donkey talked in the Bible?

Wow, that was crazy. Now imagine if donkeys could write!

Imagine no more, because we have created our very own donkey alphabet.
Use it to decode the messages from our donkey friend...maybe you will even learn
something about him!

Turn to page 118 to
find the answer key.

My Name Is DUSTY THE DONKEY

⊕ꕔ ꞁ⸱ꞁⅰ∃∩ꕔ★ ⸱ꞁⅰ∃∩ꕔ★ ᏟꝋᏟᏟ ⊕∃ ꝺ-ᏦⅠⵟⵟᏞ∃.

my FRIENDS CALL ME D-KIZZLE

Ꙇ Ꮯꝋᐯ∃ 🍎🍎Ꮯ∃★, 🌾🍌🍎🍌🍎🍌★,
🍎∩ꝺ ᗯ🍎ꞁꞁᏟ∃★.

**I LOVE APPLES, BANANAS,
AND WAFFLES**

ᗯ∩∃∩ Ꙇ ꞁᏟꝋᗯ ∪🍐 Ꙇ ᗯ🍎∩ꞁ
🥕🍠 🌾∃ 🍎∩ 🍎★🥕ꞁᏟꝋ∩🍠∪🥕.

Good work decoding those messages.
Now practice drawing the letters, and try writing your own message.

DONKEY DISAPPEAR?

No, of course not! But he did wander off on us.

Help find Donkey in all the places he's been and see if you can find things he's hidden away below.

- donkey
- cheeseburger
- pizza slice
- apple
- carrot
- strawberry
- orange
- bird
- ark
- money bag
- sheep
- frog
- ax

- palm tree
- pile of diamonds
- flashlight
- lizard
- trophy
- feather
- sword
- megaphone
- bread
- trash can
- crown

- ruler
- pencil
- hammer
- shield
- popsicle
- turtle
- steak
- guitar
- coin

Turn to page 127 to find the answer key.

JOSEPH'S ROBE OF MANY COLORS

The Bible tells us that Joseph was Jacob's favorite son (Eek—don't ask your parents who their favorite is!) and that Jacob gave him a very special coat. Different versions of the Bible describe it as...

an ornate robe • a robe of many colors • a coat of many colors • a tunic of many colors • a varicolored tunic

What do you imagine this special coat looked like?

Don't forget to bedazzle!

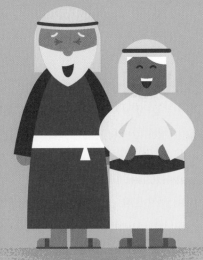

WHAT'S IN A NAME?

When the Bible tells us someone's name, sometimes it also tells us what that name means. And the meaning often reveals something about what that person was like or what God wanted them to do. God made a promise to Abram and his wife Sarai that He would build His nation through their descendants, and then God changed their names. Abram became Abraham, which means "father of many nations," and Sarai became Sarah, which means "mother of nations."

What does your name mean?

YOUR NAME:	MEANING:

What about the other members of your family?

NAME:	MEANING:
NAME:	MEANING:
NAME:	MEANING:
NAME:	MEANING:
NAME:	MEANING:
NAME:	MEANING:
NAME:	MEANING:

Do any of the meanings you discovered confirm anything about that person's character?

ZllZl...

Dreams were a major part of Joseph's story. Now, imagine if you were the one interpreting Pharaoh's dreams. Let the fun begin as you choose these words and then add them to the paraphrase on the next page!

1. _____ verb ending in -ing

2. _____ place

3. _____ body of water

4. _____ number

5. _____ animal, plural

6. _____ adjective

7. _____ adjective

8. _____ verb ending in -ed

9. _____ noun, plural

10. _____ adjective

11. _____ adjective

12. _____ adjective

13. _____ place

14. _____ verb, past tense

15. _____ noun, plural

16. _____ adjective

17. _____ adjective

18. _____ verb ending in -ing

19. _____ noun

20. _____ verb ending in -ed

21. _____ adjective

22. _____ adjective

23. _____ adjective

24. _____ noun

25. _____ verb ending in -ed

26. _____ name of a group of people

*A **verb** describes an action (such as sing, drive, gallop, or love).*

Then Pharaoh said to Joseph, "In my first dream, I was 1. _____ at 2. _____, when out of the 3. _____ there came up 4. _____ 5. _____, 6. _____ and 7. _____, and they 8. _____ among the 9. _____. After them, 4. _____ other 5. _____ came up— 10. _____ and very 11. _____ and 12. _____. I had never seen such 11. _____ 5. _____ in all the land of 13. _____. The 12. _____, 11. _____ 5. _____ 14. _____ the 4. _____, 6. _____ 5. _____ that came up first. But even after they 14. _____ them, no one could tell that they had done so; they looked just as 11. _____ as before. Then I woke up.

"In my next dream, I saw 4. _____ 15. _____, 16. _____ and 17. _____, 18. _____ on a 19. _____. After them, 4. _____ other 15. _____ 20. _____ — 21. _____ and 22. _____ and 23. _____ by the 24. _____. The 22. _____ 15. _____ 25. _____ the 4. _____ 17. _____ 15. _____. I told this to the 26. _____, but none of them could explain it to me."

...zZZ

Don't worry if it doesn't sound right—you can read the real story in Genesis 41.

A **HAIRY** SITUATION: STYLING SAMSON

Samson was pretty attached to his hair. In fact, he had strong feelings about it! Delilah learned that it was the secret of his strength, so when he fell asleep on a really bad date, she had his head shaved.

See what new hairstyle you can come up with to let Samson's locks loose again!

Check out these hairstyles for inspiration.

ITS **NOT** ABOUT THE **MONEY**

When Solomon became king, God offered to give him whatever he wanted. Solomon humbly asked for wisdom. God was so pleased; He gave him lots of wisdom—and incredible riches too!

Solomon's net worth would be about $2.2 trillion today! How many zeros are in 2.2 trillion?

$2.2 TRILLION

What would you do with $2.2 trillion?

Where would you go?

Draw your dream house.

Solomon used his wealth to build a temple for God and a palace for himself.

Fill in the blanks for your house.

	TEMPLE OF GOD	SOLOMON'S PALACE	YOUR HOME

	2,700 SQ FT	11,250 SQ FT	SQ FT = _____ (ask your parents)

SQUARE FEET IN PIZZAS

1,934 PIZZAS	**8,057** PIZZAS	How many pizzas would it take to carpet your entire your house?

Psst... 1.396 is roughly the area of a 16" pizza! Trust us on this one.

square feet [   ] ÷ **1.396** = [   ] PIZZAS

MATERIALS

Built of exotic woods, like cedar, olive, and fir, and covered in gold. The design was reminiscent of the garden of Eden.	Lined with cedar and **300** gold shields. Containers were made of gold.	What special things would you use to build a house?

I would like a house built of marshmallows.

AMENITIES

The Holy of Holies was covered in **$42 million** worth of gold.	An ivory throne overlaid with gold.	Best amenity or feature?
		TV

CROWNING ACHIEVEMENTS

Josiah was crowned king of Judah when he was only 8 years old! (Imagine someone in third grade being made king today. Whoa.)

Throughout his reign, Josiah worked actively to fight idolatry. That made him Judah's greatest king!

Maybe you'd make a great ruler too...

What would that be like?

What rules would you put in place?

No bedtimes! Par-tay all night!

What rules would you get rid of?

Who else would you put in charge? Of what?

What new holidays would you add to the calendar?

National "Ice Cream for Every Meal Day" is A. MUST.

What would you eat for a typical meal?

Marshmallows.

ROYALLY FUN POP QUIZ

A kingdom of questions for quizzically inclined minds! See how much you know about the famous (and infamous!) kings of Israel (the northern kingdom) and Judah (the southern kingdom).

1. Who anointed Saul as king?

A Jesus

B Isaiah

C Abraham

D Samuel

2. David defeated Goliath with a...

A sword

B banjo

C sling

D formal invite to his annual summer BBQ

3. What would Solomon's net worth be today?

A 3 goats and 5 pigs

B $2.2 trillion

C 1 vault full of gold

D 80 Ferraris and one food cart

4. How old was Joash when he was crowned king?

A 7 years old

B 18 months old

C 77 years old

D 600 years old

E He'd rather not say—it's a sensitive topic.

5. Josiah was considered...

A Judah's greatest king

B the world's best break dancer

C a brilliant artist, ahead of his time

D Jesus's greatest disciple

6. Zedekiah was the prophet Jeremiah's...

A grandson

B valet

C cousin

D Uber driver

7. Ahab was considered Israel's _____ king.

A funniest

B worst

C best

D silliest

E best-looking

8. Jeroboam II was Israel's _____ king.

A shortest-reigning

B kindest

C longest-reigning

D worst-smelling

E angriest

Turn to page 121 to find the answer key.

LOGICALLY THE MOST FUN

The kings (and 1 queen) of Israel and Judah reigned for a total of 414 years. A few accomplished many great things for God's kingdom, but most had lots of huge failures. (Ouch...but true.)

It might help to know some of those kings better. You're in charge of figuring out which **king** is the **son** of which king, what **era** he reigned in, and who was the **prophet** at the time.

Directions

1 Use the clues to solve the puzzle. Use the chart on the next page to keep track.

2 Mark an X where you know there's a wrong answer, and a ✓ where you know there's a right answer.

3 Use the process of elimination to help narrow down the answers.

Read the verses—the Bible will give you the help you need!

Clues

1 Amon's son, the youngest king of Judah (who was only 8 years old when he became king), reigned in 640 BC (2 Kings 22:1).

2 The most recent king was the last king in Jesus's family line. Jeremiah prophesied that none of his offspring would rule in Judah (Jeremiah 22:24-30).

3 Omri's son, known as Israel's worst king, reigned during the time of the prophet Elijah (1 Kings 22:37-40).

4 Nathan was prophet during the time that this father and son reigned during the united kingdom of Israel, before the kingdoms divided in 930 BC (1 Kings 2:10-12).

Read the clues very carefully (and more than once!). Many clues have more than one hidden answer to help.

Turn to page 123 to find the answer key.

⁉

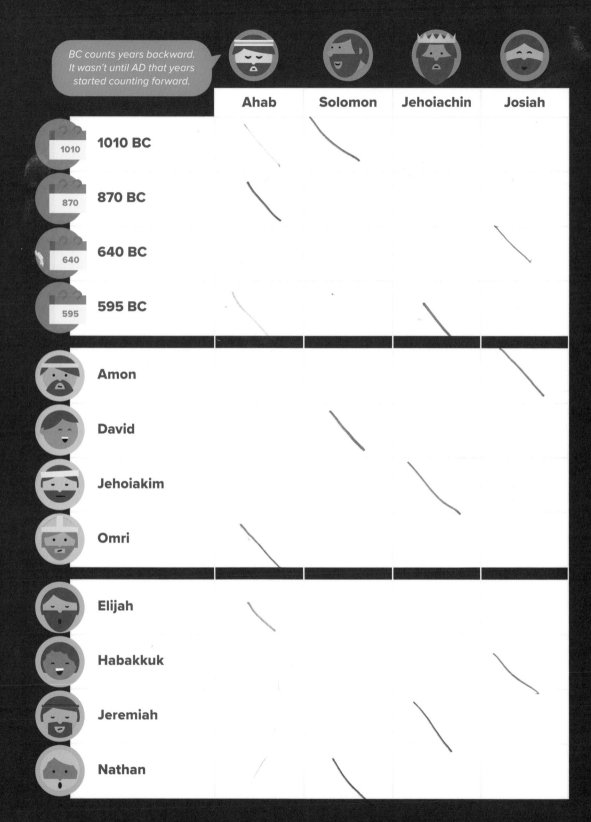

WORDS OF PSALMS

Psalms is a book full of praise for God. Ever wonder what words show up the most often in Psalms? Find them below!

LORD	HAND	MAN	SING	THANKS
GOD	EARTH	WICKED	ENDURES	RIGHTEOUS
LOVE	NAME	DAY	GREAT	CHILDREN
STEADFAST	PRAISE	PEOPLE	RIGHT	EVIL
HEART	SOUL	GIVE	FEAR	FOREVER

```
N Z V I Z W J G D C H T R A E
E E S V L N D H D S K M X B E
G V V F E A R S E R U D N E M
C H I L D R E N W A U L J F A
I S E G Y L D I Z Q R E P E N
A K G D O N C L D U X T V A G
Y N N A M K J R H P E O P L E
X A X K E D O G O R L C G B P
H H D D K L T K Q N X N E T R
S T E A D F A S T P I I A V A
O R E V E R O F R S K E C K I
U K Y O E V I L C B R Z Y M S
L Q Z S U O E T H G I R D P E
S L W T H G I R X K V Z U G X
X A Z T W I V F N L O O Q L H
```

Turn to page 122 to find the answer key.

What's your favorite verse from the Psalms? Write it here:

Does your favorite verse use any of the words in the word search? Which ones?

THE WISDOM OF PROVERBS

While writing the book of Proverbs, King Solomon misplaced his notes. Help him match up the pieces of wisdom.

1. **Proverbs 3:5**—Trust in the LORD with all your ⬚⬚⬚ .

2. **Proverbs 4:23**—Above all else, ⬚⬚⬚ your heart.

3. **Proverbs 27:17**—As iron ⬚⬚⬚ iron...

4. **Proverbs 5:4**—...sharp as a double-edged ⬚⬚⬚ .

5. **Proverbs 16:18**— ⬚⬚⬚ goes before destruction.

6. **Proverbs 26:1**—Like snow in ⬚⬚⬚ ...

7. **Proverbs 9:10**— The fear of the LORD is the beginning of ⬚⬚⬚ .

8. **Proverbs 17:22**—A cheerful heart is good ⬚⬚⬚ .

9. **Proverbs 15:1**—A gentle answer turns away ⬚⬚⬚ .

10. **Proverbs 3:6**—In all your ways submit to him, and he will make your ⬚⬚⬚ .

11. **Proverbs 17:17**—A friend ⬚⬚⬚ at all times.

12. **Proverbs 3:1**—Keep my ⬚⬚⬚ in your heart.

medicine

commands

heart

wrath

loves

guard

sharpens

sword

pride

paths straight

summer

wisdom

Check your answers by looking up the verses in your Bible!
If you don't have an NIV handy, find the answer key on page 119.

WHICH **EMPIRE** DO THESE **BELONG** TO?

What better way to impress your friends than to know a little Babylonian history? Well, knowing some things about the Romans, obviously!

But why stop there? You may as well learn something about the empires of Persia and Greece too. (That sounds so fancy!)

Trust us, your friends will be in awe.

Draw a line from the object/person/event to the empire it belongs to!

1 **King Cyrus**

2 **Queen Esther**

3 **Alexander the Great**

4 **Julius Ceasar**

5 **kidnapped Daniel from Judah**

6 **the Olympics**

7 **worshipped Jupiter**

8 **the Magi**

9 **King Nebuchadnezzar**

10 **established one of the earliest democracies**

11 **built extensive roads**

12 **the Hanging Gardens**

13 **threw Daniel in a lions' den**

14 **worshipped Zeus**

15 **King Darius**

Babylon

Persia

Greece

Rome

Turn to page 120 to find the answer key.

readiness

family protection

learning and listening

safety

peace

determination

intelligence

faith

love and devotion

service to the church

Christianity

strength and valor

wisdom

plenty

hope

glory

honor in battle

courage

Some families proudly display a crest, or a "coat of arms." Crests are usually in the shape of a shield and have various symbols on them that can mean different things.

Design a crest for your family to display in your kingdom.

WHAT'S THE DEAL WITH THE TABERNACLE?

The Tabernacle. Hard to understand but fun to learn more about!

Search for words below that help bring better understanding to "God's dwelling place."

AARON	CHURCH	FIRE	MANNA	TABERNACLE
ALTAR	COMMANDMENTS	GOLD	MOSES	TABLETS
ARK	COVENANT	HOLY	SACRIFICE	TEMPLE
ATONEMENT	DWELLING	JERUSALEM	SMOKE	TENT
BREAD	EDEN	LAMPSTAND	SOLOMON	VEIL

```
W H G B F L S Q E P O D Y V E
M P C A H O T C L R E N K E E
K E R R L A I N P C R A D I Q
N K L O U F D Z M O I T W L T
X E M A I H S G E M F S E Y H
X O D R S N C A T M T P L N U
N O C E O U U L V A Y M L M T
J A P R V Y R T B N Q A I A I
S Q A H O L Y E D D F L N N O
H A L T A R R M J M B K G N A
T N E M E N O T A E K R A A T
V V U D A S R K H N W D E E V
C C L C E P Y V S T E L B A T
C O L S H Y V J A S P Q V C D
G E C O V E N A N T E K O M S
```

Turn to page 122 to find the answer key.

For comparison, draw yourself and the height of your friends or family members compared to Og.

Who is Og? Read Deuteronomy 3.

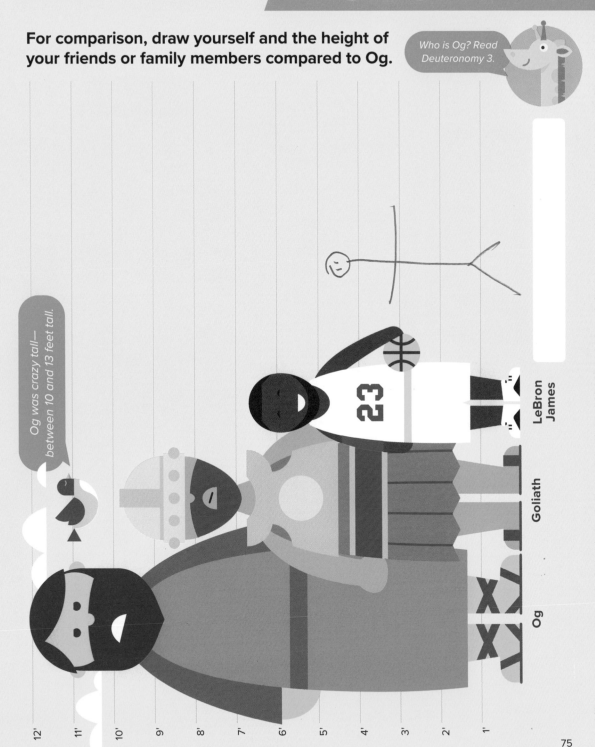

Og was crazy tall—between 10 and 13 feet tall.

LeBron James

Goliath

Og

12' 11' 10' 9' 8' 7' 6' 5' 4' 3' 2' 1'

IT'S **OKAY** TO BE **DIFFERENT** (EXCEPT IN THIS GAME)

Spot the difference between the pictures of Bible heroes and villains!

There are 6 differences each!

ESTHER
The Brave Queen

GOLIATH
The Warrior Giant

JOSEPH
The Shepherd Dreamer

CAIN
The First Murderer

JOSEPH
The Sheepy Dreamer

CAIN
The First Brother

ESTHER
The Bravest Queen

GOLIATH
The Warrior King

Turn to page 125 to find the answer key.

God has a purpose for YOU!

Create your own, personal, hero trading card—infographic style.

Give your infographic identity some extra character—smiling eyes, rosy cheeks, a fun hat, interesting clothes...

THE BEST OF ME:

MY FUTURE JOB:

FAVORITE ACTIVITY:

FAVORITE BIBLE HERO:

FAVORITE BIBLE VERSE:

NAME:

Future Award Winner

A **LANDMARK** OCCASION

The Bible talks about really cool landmarks. Remember Noah's Ark and Mount Ararat?

What are some cool landmarks where you live?

Draw something from outside!

That's the place you go when you leave your house and put away electronics.

Draw a building, your house, or a neat-looking structure that you know really well, or might even be famous where you live. Maybe add your own design touches too!

Why don't we install extra-large donuts on the top of more buildings?

Find a mountain or a **REALLY** big hill near you *(or a landmark you really love...Mount Rushmore, anyone?)* and fill it in next to the ones mentioned.

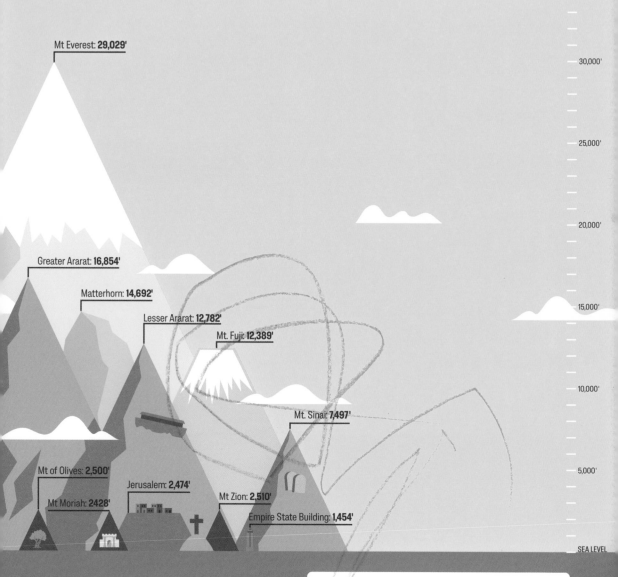

Mt Everest: **29,029'**

Greater Ararat: **16,854'**

Matterhorn: **14,692'**

Lesser Ararat: **12,782'**

Mt. Fuji: **12,389'**

Mt. Sinai: **7,497'**

Mt of Olives: **2,500'**

Jerusalem: **2,474'**

Mt Moriah: **2428'**

Mt Zion: **2,510'**

Empire State Building: **1,454'**

35,000'
30,000'
25,000'
20,000'
15,000'
10,000'
5,000'
SEA LEVEL

How tall is the landmark you drew?

Have you climbed a mountain or big hill? How long did it take?

WONDER DOUGH

The people in Bible times built some pretty incredible structures. The Roman Colosseum could hold about 50,000 spectators, which is about the same as Yankee Stadium.

Okay, so actually building the Roman Colosseum might not be possible for you, but you could try making it out of wonder dough.

Here's a recipe!

Ingredients

1 cup all-purpose flour
½ cup salt
2 tsps. cream of tartar

1 cup warm water
1 T. vegetable oil
food coloring

Wow, that is a LOT of salt!

Instructions

1. Mix the dry ingredients together in a large pot.

2. Add water and oil.

3. Cook over medium heat, stirring constantly, until it starts to look like mashed potatoes.

Yumm, mashed potatoes!

4. Remove the mixture from the stovetop and divide it into balls.

5. Allow it to cool. Then add food coloring and knead it until it's smooth.

Divide your dough into balls and create all the colors of the rainbow!

You can store this wonder dough for up to 3 months in an airtight container or the Ark of the Covenant. (We recommend an airtight container.)

Now you try...

THE GREAT
PYRAMID
OF GIZA

THE ROMAN
COLOSSEUM

THE LIGHTHOUSE
OF ALEXANDRIA

MAKE A **MENORAH**

The lampstand (or menorah) in the Tabernacle and Temple was a candlestick with 7 branches.

The branches symbolized the tree of life from the Garden of Eden. The fire represented God's presence and was a continual reminder that God wanted to dwell with humanity.

Let's make our own!

Supplies

paper plate
7 miniature craft sticks
1 jumbo craft stick
yellow and orange paper

scissors
markers or paint
white craft glue
paper cup

Instructions

1. With scissors, cut the paper plate in half. Color one of the halves however you like. The more colorful and elaborate, the better! Draw the candle holders on it, like in the image on the right.

2. Decorate the miniature craft sticks. These will be our candlesticks.

3. Glue one of the miniature craft sticks in the center of the plate on the cut side. Glue the remaining craft sticks slightly lower than the center one, three on each side. Don't forget to let the glue dry—sticky fingers are no joke!

4. Glue the jumbo craft stick in the center at the bottom of the plate.

5. Cut yellow and orange paper into the shape of candle flames. If you don't have colored paper, you can use regular white printer paper and color it. Glue the flames to the ends of the craft sticks.

6. Carefully stick the jumbo craft stick into an upside-down paper cup to make a pedestal for the menorah.

7. Set the lampstand on a table for all to see!

NATIVITY SPOT THE DIFFERENCES

Jesus is born! Carefully compare these two scenes and spot the 20 differences!

Turn to page 126 to find the answer key.

A STAR IS BORN

You'll need...

star paper on pages 139 and 141

glue or tape

mind ready to learn

fingers ready to fold

Let's start with sheet #1, page 139

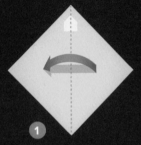

1

Fold the right side over to the left side, crease down the middle.

2

Fold this top flap over so the blue edge meets the orange edge.

(colored edges for guide only)

3

Flip the whole thing over!

4

Fold the bottom up to meet the top.

It should look like this now!

Move on to the next step.

The Pin & Pull (non-technical name)

This is the trickiest part...so I'll break it down in slow-motion.

> Master this, and you are on your way to becoming a paper-folding sensei.

Press down here, pinning your creation to the table

5

Grab the corner of this flap and pull it down toward you.

6

As you pull this down, the flap will lift up off the table, creating what looks like a pocket.

7

Keep pulling the flap down.

In order to complete this part you will need creases, marked by the dashed lines.

(transparency for guide only)

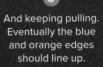

8

And keeping pulling. Eventually the blue and orange edges should line up.

(colored edges for guide only)

See what I mean?!

Time for sheet #2, page 141

9 Fold the bottom up to meet the top.

10 Fold the right side to meet up with the left.

11 You'll have this now, but let's rotate it so it looks like an upside-down pyramid.

12 Fold the tip back at the dotted line on the paper.

Ok, let's put it all together!

13 Place the Kinda Cool shape from Part 2...

14 ...between the layers of the cool arrow from Part 1.

15 Like this!
Glue, or tape it in place.

VOILÀ

Now you have a star, just a super sweet, paper star!

Spot and See:

Stare at the star for 30 seconds and then close your eyes—you can still see it!

WISE MAN MAZE

Help the wise men find their way to Jesus.

Along the way, find and collect the three gifts they brought him.

Gold	
Frankincense	
Myrrh	

Turn to page 124 to find the solution.

GOSPEL GOODNESS MATCHING GAME

So many Gospels, so little time. Matthew, Mark, Luke, John—which of the four Gospel writers are known for the things below?

Turn to page 119 to find the answer key.

1. "He said to them, 'Go into all the world and preach the gospel to all creation.'"

2. tax collector

3. his Gospel is least like the other three

4. doctor

5. "Peace I leave with you; my peace I give you. I do not give to you as the world gives. Do not let your hearts be troubled and do not be afraid."

6. evangelist

7. "Therefore go and make disciples of all nations, baptizing them in the name of the Father and of the Son and of the Holy Spirit."

8. also known as Levi

9. fisherman

10. wrote the longest Gospel and New Testament book

11. "Love the Lord your God with all your heart and with all your soul and with all your mind and with all your strength."

12. Barnabas's relative

13. "Then Jesus came to them and said, 'All authority in heaven and on earth has been given to me.'"

14. "For God so loved the world that he gave his one and only Son, that whoever believes in him shall not perish but have eternal life."

15. "For the Son of Man came to seek and to save the lost."

16. "The angel said to her, 'Do not be afraid, Mary; you have found favor with God. You will conceive and give birth to a son, and you are to call him Jesus.'"

Matthew

Mark

Luke

John

JESUS: THE GOD-MAN

Jesus has two natures—truly and fully God, and truly and fully man. Yet Jesus is only one person.

Whoa.

Draw lines to match the descriptions to what reflects Jesus's humanity or His divinity.

Turn to page 120 to find the answer key.

He is able to forgive sins

He bled and died

He is all-powerful

He cried

He breathed air

He was tired

He is sovereign

DIVINITY

HUMANITY

He is eternal, living before He became a human

He received worship from his followers

He is present everywhere

He wasn't glamorous or notable in appearance

He is all-knowing

He grew from a baby to an adult

He was hungry and thirsty

CRACK THE CODE

Some letters have been taken out of these verses and placed in a jumbled mess.

Yikes.

See if you can figure out what these two important verses are saying about Jesus.

E I A N C O H I R E P R D A U I
Y A M N O C D O F T E E I A T

"H_ __s t_ _ r_d_ _ _ _e _ _ _h_ gl_ _ _ of G_ _ a_ _ the _x_ _t _ _ _ _int of h_s n_ _ _re."

Hebrews 1:3 ESV

Use the Bible verses to help!

N B I D E A T O A V D M I I E S N U
N E D B L M N R U M M E C I O E O

"A_ _ _ _ _ng f_ _nd in hu_ _ _ fo_ _, he h_ _ _ _ _ed hi_ _ _lf by b_ _om_ _g obe_ _ _ _ _t to the p_ _nt of de_ _h, e_en _ _ath on a cr_ ss."

Philippians 2:8 ESV

Turn to page 118 to find the answer key.

JESUS'S FAMILY TREE

Step 1—Help Jesus find all his family members.
When you find one of these names, draw a line through it.

ABRAHAM	ENOSH	JOSEPH	NOAH	SHEM
ADAM	ISAAC	JOSIAH	RAHAB	SOLOMON
BATHSHEBA	JACOB	LEVI	REHOBOAM	TAMAR
DAVID	JESSE	MARY	RUTH	
ENOCH	JEHOIACHIN	METHUSELAH	SETH	

```
E S U S T A M A R R I S T
E N O C H H J O S E P H S
E S O M R U T H O H N O O
F J J A E G O D B O T A L
L O E E H T H E A B S B O
E S H O N B H N T O S R M
V I O O A O F U H A E A O
I A I H J M S S S M T H N
I H A A E D J H H E H A N
S R C A S A A E E M L M M
A N H D S V C M B T A A H
A E I S E I O O A N D R H
C O N F D D B A V A I D Y
```

Turn to page 122 to find the answer key.

Step 2—Write down all the remaining letters here to reveal who Jesus really is!

To find the hidden message, look for unmarked letters. Start in the top left and follow along the rows to the right just like you read a book.

Hidden Message: "J _ _ _ _ _   _ _ _   _ _ _

_ _ _   _ _ _   _ _ _ _ ,   _ _ _   _ _ _ _

_ _ _ ,   _ _ _ _ _   _ _ _ _ _ _   _ _ _ _ _ _ _ !"

92

JESUS'S FAMILY HISTORY

Can you piece together the keys to Jesus's family history? Draw a line to match each name to what they are known for.

Turn to page 119 to find the answer key.

1	the first man	David
2	survived the great flood	Solomon
3	obeyed God by being willing to sacrifice his son Isaac	Judah
4	tricked his father into giving him the blessing of the firstborn, which belonged to his brother Esau	Mary
5	tribe of Israel that Jesus belonged to	Joseph
6	a man after God's own heart (Acts 13:22)	Methuselah
7	the richest and wisest man who ever lived (1 Kings 10:23)	Abraham
8	Judah's greatest king—only 8 years old when he became king	Adam
9	father of Jesus	Jacob
10	gave birth to a son and named him Immanuel	Rahab
11	helped the spies in Jericho	Josiah
12	Methuselah's father—he never died! (Genesis 5:21-24)	Noah
13	the oldest person on record (Noah's grandfather), living to be 969 years old	Enoch

BREAD OF LIFE RECIPE

Ingredients

4 cups bread flour
1½ cups warm water
1½ tsps. fast-action dry yeast

1 T. olive oil
1 tsp. salt
1 T. sugar

Directions

1 Combine all the ingredients except the water and oil into a large bowl. Create a large hole in the flour like it's a giant crater!

2 Pour the water and oil into the crater. Mix it up until there's no dry flour left. Place the dough on a lightly floured surface.

3 Knead the dough for about 5 minutes.
If you need help, get your parents and siblings involved!

4 Form the dough into a round shape.
It should look like a slightly smushed basketball.

5 Place the dough in a warm place for 1 hour.
The dough is going to grow to almost twice its size!

Imagine if you grew that fast. How tall would you be? ____ ' ____ " Okay, back to baking.

6 While the dough is still resting and rising, ask your parents to preheat the oven to 450 degrees.
Be careful; the oven can be dangerous!

7 Place the dough on a greased baking tray and have your parents slide it into the oven. Bake for 20-25 minutes.

Right before placing the dough into the oven, you can decorate the dough with something fun like raisins or M&M's.

8 Once it's ready, ask your parents to take the bread out of the oven.
Let the bread cool before touching it! It's going to be very hot.

9 Once the bread has cooled, enjoy it! Feel free to spread some butter or jam on it (or fig jelly). Maybe you can make it into a delicious sandwich!

BRING ME SOME **FIGGY JELLY**

You've probably read about figs in the Bible, but maybe you've never tasted one. Try this tasty fig jelly recipe!

Ingredients

rind of one lemon
¾ cup granulated sugar
2 T. honey
1½ T. lemon juice
1 or 2 sprigs thyme
1 lb. ripe fresh figs, stemmed and quartered

Directions

1. Use a vegetable peeler to remove strips of rind from the lemon.

2. Place all the ingredients into a saucepan and stir them together.

3. Boil over medium-high heat, stirring frequently. Reduce heat to medium-low and simmer 40 to 50 minutes or until the mixture thickens. *Continue to stir frequently so the mixture doesn't stick to the bottom of the pot.*

4. Discard the thyme stems and lemon peel. Use a blender to chop up the fig skins (if desired).

5. Pour into an 8-ounce jelly jar. *Keep refrigerated for up to one month.*

Ways to enjoy your fig jelly!

Spread it on toast or an English muffin

Add it to ice cream

Try it on pancakes instead of syrup

Make homemade Fig Newtons

Spread it on a grilled ham-and-cheese sandwich

4 GOSPELS, 18 QUESTIONS, ALL GOOD NEWS

The four Gospels give a wonderful portrait of Jesus and His ministry. They include everything from His birth to His crucifixion and resurrection! Use the clues below to test out your knowledge and reveal an important hidden message!

Clues:

1 This Gospel shows a much different picture of Jesus than the other three.

2 Luke is the _____ Gospel. (It's also the wordiest book in the New Testament.)

3 The Gospels are the first four books in this section of the Bible.

4 There are _____ Gospels.

5 The 12 disciples (and a few others) were also known as _____ , which means they were messengers.

6 Matthew introduces Jesus as the _____ , the one who the Hebrew Bible promised would deliverer the Jewish nation.

7 "Gospel" means "_____ _____ ."

8 Jesus called the Messiah, or _____ , which can mean "Anointed One."

9 Mark is the _____ Gospel. (It's quick and action packed!)

10 Matthew went by this name before meeting Jesus.

11 Mark is known as an _____ , a person who works to bring others to Christianity.

12 Luke practiced this profession before starting to follow Jesus.

13 The Gospels tell us Jesus is the _____ of God.

14 The Gospels show the fulfillment of prophecies from this section of the Bible.

15 Matthew, Mark, and Luke are sometimes known as the _____ Gospels.

16 Before Matthew became a disciple, he was a _____ _____ .

17 _____ is the only Gospel that mentions the Wise Men (the Magi).

18 The Gospels cover the life, death, and resurrection of _____ .

Hidden Message:

_ _ _ _ _ _   _ _ _

_ _ _ _ _   _ _ _ _ _ _   _ _ _ _ _ _

Turn to page 120 to find the answer key.

FISHY MONEY

In Matthew 17:27, Jesus tells Peter to go fishing, and that in the mouth of the first fish he catches, he'll find a coin to pay a tax. What are the odds!

Help Peter find his way though the fish maze to reach the coin.

Right on the nose. In 2002, a man caught a swordfish, put his wedding ring on its nose, and released it. Incredibly, three years later, he caught the same swordfish—and it still had the ring on its nose!

Turn to page 124 to find the solution.

WATCH A SEED GROW

Jesus said that the kingdom of God is like a seed. It starts off small, but then it grows and grows with new life!

Let's plant our own seeds and see how they grow.

Supplies

bush bean seeds
a container (at least 4 inches tall)
soil (if you can, use loose soil mixed with compost!)

Instructions

1 Fill your container with soil. Make sure the dirt is loose and not packed tightly.

2 Plant your seeds about 1 inch deep into the soil. Make sure each seed is about 2 inches apart from other seeds so they have room to spread their roots!

3 Lightly water the seeds until the soil is damp. Don't water the seeds so that the water gets muddy! Bush bean seeds don't need a lot of water. Just make sure the soil does not dry out. Try to water your seeds every morning.

4 Place the container in a place where the seeds can receive at least 8 hours of sunlight a day. A windowsill should be the perfect place.

5 Wait and watch for your seeds to grow!

Once the shoots are about 3 inches tall, you can transplant them to larger containers and move them outdoors.

JESUS SAVES

Use the clues to reveal important words related to the most important act (ever!): Jesus dying for our sins!

Clues:

1 Jesus said He would be killed and then, on the _____ day, be raised to life (Matthew 16:21).

2 The event we celebrate on Easter and the apostles testified about (Acts 4:33).

3 This pierced Jesus's side as He hung on the cross (John 19:34).

4 The site of Jesus's crucifixion ("the place of the Skull," a.k.a. Calvary) (John 19:17).

5 Jesus is the Son of _____ (Luke 22:70).

6 Jesus is also "the _____ of Man" (Matthew 26:64).

7 They mocked Jesus on the cross, offering Him wine and vinegar (Luke 23:36-37).

8 Jesus entered Jerusalem riding on a _____ (Matthew 21:1-11).

9 The disciple who betrayed Jesus (Matthew 27:3).

10 Our name for the meal Jesus shared with His disciples (Mark 14:12-26).

11 The day we celebrate Jesus's triumphal entry into Jerusalem (John 12:12-18).

12 The Roman governor who convicted Jesus, leading to His crucifixion (John 18:28-40).

13 Jesus's last words on the cross (John 19:30).

14 He was crucified for our sins and resurrected (Acts 10:39-43).

15 The number of men (thieves) crucified next to Jesus (Luke 23:32).

16 The people Jesus came to save—another way of saying everybody (1 Timothy 2:5).

17 Jesus was crucified on a _____ (Philippians 2:8).

18 This was placed on Jesus's head at His crucifixion (Matthew 27:29).

19 He helped Jesus carry the cross (Matthew 27:32).

Turn to page 121 to find the answer key.

PROPHECY MATCHING

The Old Testament includes more than 186 prophecies about the coming Messiah, and Jesus fulfilled every single one of them! Pretty impressive.

Here are just a handful of the prophecies. See if you can match the **Old Testament prophecy** about the Messiah to its **New Testament fulfillment** in Jesus. Look up the New Testament verses and draw a line to the Old Testament prophecy it corresponds to.

Read carefully because some are tricky!

Turn to page 120 to find the answer key.

OLD TESTAMENT PROPHECY

1. **descendant of King David**
   2 Samuel 7:12-16

2. **born in Bethlehem**
   Micah 5:2

3. **born of a virgin**
   Isaiah 7:14

4. **teaches in parables**
   Psalm 78:1-2

5. **rides into Jerusalem on a donkey**
   Zechariah 9:9

6. **betrayed by a close friend**
   Psalm 41:9

7. **hands and feet are pierced**
   Psalm 22:15-16

8. **no bones are broken**
   Psalm 34:19-20

9. **rises from the dead**
   Psalm 16:10-11

10. **ascends to heaven and sits at God's right hand** • Psalm 68:18

NEW TESTAMENT FULFILLMENT

- John 13:18
- Matthew 1:22-23
- Matthew 2:1
- Matthew 21:1-11
- John 19:33-36
- Mark 16:5-6
- Luke 1:32
- Acts 1:9-11
- John 20:25-27
- Matthew 13:34-35

ODDS EXPERIMENT

When you flip a coin there is a **1 in 2 chance** you'll get heads up. Pretty simple, right?

Well, things get a lot harder if you want to get heads several times in a row. The odds of getting heads 10 times in a row is **1 in 1,024**. But get this, the probability of getting heads 50 times in a row is **1 in 1,125,899,906,842,624**. That's still better odds than 1 person fulfilling just 8 of the prophecies about the Messiah, which is **1 in 100,000,000,000,000,000** (that's ONE in a hundred quadrillion!). And Jesus fulfilled over 150 prophecies!

Flip a coin 100 times and keep track of your results below marking each time you get heads.

Those are some big numbers.

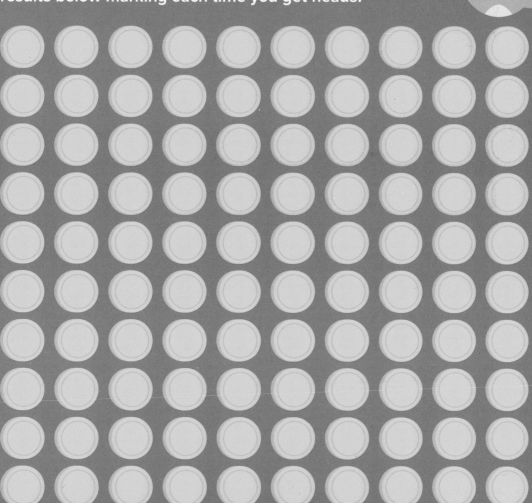

ON GUARD!

After Jesus was crucified, He was buried in a tomb. At least 4 Roman soldiers guarded the tomb. On the third day, there was a violent earthquake, and an angel of the Lord rolled away the stone from the tomb's entrance and sat on it.

This terrified the Roman soldiers!

Before they run off, see if you can color in the picture to see what the guards looked like on duty.

YTINIRT

Bible scholars have been studying the doctrine of the Trinity for more than 2,000 years! We may not have that much time, so we'll stick to the basics.

Unscramble the words below that describe the Trinity!

1 RTHFAE

2 NSO

3 RIIPTS

4 NEO

5 LAQEU

6 CISTNTDI

Bonus scramble!

See if you can unscramble these big words describing common misconceptions about the Trinity. If you need help, check out page 43 in *Bible Infographics for Kids, Volume 2* (sold separately).

1 **EISITRHTM** *Clue: The belief that there are three gods, not one God.*

2 **RMINASAI** *Clue: The belief that Jesus and the Spirit are not fully God.*

3 **SLOMAIMD** *Clue: The belief that the Father, Son, and Spirit are just different names for God.*

Turn to page 119 to find the answer key.

TRINITY COLOR BY NUMBER

Understanding the Trinity might be challenging (after all, like we said, Bible scholars have been studying the doctrine for more than 2,000 years), but coloring in each section according to the number below might help bring a little more understanding.

FATHER 1 2 3 **SON** 4 5 6 **SPIRIT** 7 8 9

KICKS FOR JESUS

Paul spread the Good News of Jesus far and wide, traveling more than 10,000 miles! If you were to walk that distance, you would likely burn through **25 pairs of shoes!**

Design your own gospel-spreading shoes!

"Stand firm...with your feet fitted with the readiness that comes from the gospel of peace"

Ephesians 6:14-15

Paul wrote almost half of the books in the New Testament.

Unscramble the words to discover which ones.

1 **UTITS**

2 **YMTITOH**

3 **SPINLHAIPIP**

4 **OHNMPLEI**

5 **ISOSLSOCAN**

6 **HASPESEIN**

7 **MRSOAN**

8 **ONSNITCARIH**

9 **TSOILSANNASEH**

10 **TALNSAIAG**

THE CHURCH

The church is important for Christ followers. There we learn about Jesus, worship Him, and get to know other Christians.

Tell us a little bit about your church!

What is the name of your church?

Where is it?

How long have you been going to it?

What's your favorite part about the church?

What are some of the names of your church leaders?

Draw one of your church leaders.

Draw your church building.

Unfortunately, many Christians around the world do not get to worship Jesus in a free country. The countries they live in make laws against attending church, and they throw Christians in jail.

One of the best things we can do for our fellow Christians is to pray for those who are being persecuted.

Here are some things we can be praying about:

THE COUNTRIES WITH THE MOST PERSECUTION ARE...

North Korea **1**

Iran **9**   **2** Afghanistan

Libya **4**   **5** Pakistan

Sudan **7**   **10** India

Eritrea **6**   **8** Yemen

3 Somalia

EVERY WEEK, 182 CHURCHES ARE ATTACKED.

EVERY MONTH, 309 CHRISTIANS ARE PUT IN PRISON FOR THEIR FAITH.

ABOUT 260 MILLION CHRISTIANS ARE UNDER THREAT OF HIGH TO SEVERE LEVELS OF PERSECUTION.

Other things you can do:

- Start a bake sale or a lemonade stand and donate the money to buy Bibles for persecuted countries.

- Gather a group of friends to pray for persecuted Christians every week.

- Pick a different country to pray for each day.

- Ask your church leaders to support missionaries overseas.

Write your own ideas:

Open Doors USA, "World Watch List 2020," https://www.opendoorsusa.org/wp-content/uploads/2020/01/2020_World_Watch_List.pdf.

FINDING **FRUIT** OF THE **SPIRIT**

In John 15, we learn that Jesus is the vine and we are the branches. Apart from God we can do nothing, but with Him we can bear fruit. Find all the fruit!

Unscramble the letters you find on each fruit to reveal the fruit of the Spirit is...

4 _ _ _ _

3 _ _ _

5 _ _ _ _ _

8 _ _ _ _ _ _ _ _

8 _ _ _ _ _ _ _ _

8 _ _ _ _ _ _ _ _

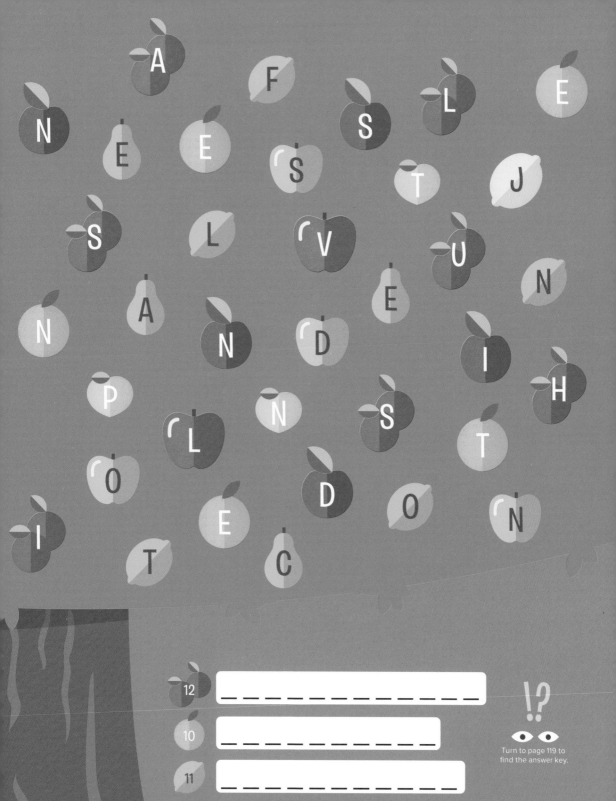

Turn to page 119 to find the answer key.

FRUITY (OF THE SPIRIT) SMOOTHIES

Directions for any of the recipes below

1. Place all the ingredients in a blender.
2. Blend until smooth!
3. Pour into cups or glasses.
4. Enjoy!

Don't forget to put the lid on the blender!

Each recipe makes two big smoothies or four little ones.
But who wants a little smoothie? No one.

For the Love of Lime

3 cups frozen pineapple
1 cup full-fat coconut milk
2 tsp. lime zest
2 T. lime juice

Jolly Joy

1½ cups cherry juice
1 banana
1½ cups frozen dark sweet cherries
¾ cup vanilla yogurt

Peace and Carrots

1 cup carrots, shredded
1 banana
1 cup mango chunks
1½ cups orange juice

Peary Patience

2 pears, cored and chopped
1 banana
1 cup milk
½ cup yogurt (vanilla or plain)
½ tsp. ground cinnamon
1 pinch nutmeg

Strawberry Kiwi **Kindness**

1 banana
½ cup strawberries
1 kiwi
½ cup vanilla frozen yogurt
¾ cup pineapple orange juice

Peanut Butter **Goodness**

2 bananas
1 cup frozen pineapple chunks
1 cup ice
1½ cups coconut milk
¼ cup peanut butter
¼ cup vanilla yogurt
1 T. honey

Grape **Gentleness**

½ cup plain yogurt
¼ cup grape juice
2 cups red seedless grapes
1 cup ice

Fruity **Faithfulness**

Layer 1:
  1 cup frozen raspberries
  1 banana
  1 cup coconut milk

Layer 2:
  1 cup frozen mango chunks
  1½ cups pineapple juice
  1 tsp. vanilla extract

Blend each layer separately. Pour the mango layer over the raspberry layer!

Chocolate Strawberry **Self-Control**

1 cup frozen strawberries
1 frozen banana
1 cup chocolate milk
1 T. unsweetened cocoa powder

DOT-TO-DOT SERAPHIM

Connect the numbered dots below to discover the seraphim.

When you're all done, add your own details or color it in!

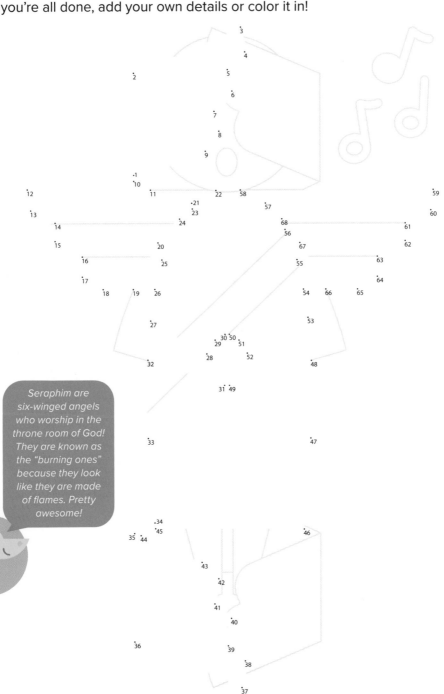

Seraphim are six-winged angels who worship in the throne room of God! They are known as the "burning ones" because they look like they are made of flames. Pretty awesome!

ANGELCOPTER

Make your very own angel that flies through the air like a helicopter!

Supplies

scissors
paperclip
angel cutout from page 135

Instructions

1. Cut out the angel design on page 135.

2. Inside the angel design, cut along the solid lines only (not the dotted ones).

3. Fold one of the wings to one side along the dotted line and fold the other wing the opposite direction.

4. Fold the two long flaps toward the middle.

5. Fold the bottom section up along the dotted line.

6. Paperclip the bottom section and the flaps all together.

7. Toss the angel up into the air and watch it fly!

Every time you follow these instructions, an angel get its wings.

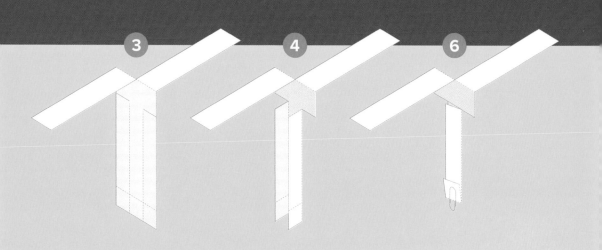

!? THE ANSWER KEY

IT'S ALL GREEK TO ME!

1. In the beginning God created the heavens and the earth.

2. For God so loved the world that he gave his one and only Son, that whoever believes in him shall not perish but have eternal life.

3. The new testament also was written without verse numbers, chapter numbers, or section headings. These were added later to help readers like you.

4. What's your favorite flavor of ice cream? Write out the answer below.

DONKEY DECODER

1. My name is Dusty Donkey.

2. My friends call me D-kizzle.

3. I love apples, bananas, and waffles.

4. When I grow up I want to be an astronaut.

THE PLAGUES OF EGYPT

1. BLOOD

2. FROGS

3. GNATS

4. FLIES

5. LIVESTOCK

6. BOILS

7. HAIL

8. LOCUSTS

9. DARKNESS

10. FIRSTBORN

CRACK THE CODE

Hebrews 1:3: He is the radiance of the glory of God and the exact imprint of his nature.

Philippians 2:8: And being found in human form, he humbled himself by becoming obedient to the point of death, even death on a cross.

YTINIRT

1. FATHER
2. SON
3. SPIRIT
4. ONE
5. EQUAL
6. DISTINCT

BONUS 1: TRITHEISM
BONUS 2: ARIANISM
BONUS 3: MODALISM

BY PAUL THE APOSTLE

1. Titus
2. Timothy
3. Philippians
4. Philemon
5. Colossians
6. Ephesians
7. Romans
8. Corinthians
9. Thessalonians
10. Galatians

FINDING FRUIT OF THE SPIRIT

red apples — love
lemons — joy
pears — peace

peaches — patience
plums — kindness
green apples — goodness

cherries — faithfulness
oranges — gentleness
limes — self-control

THE WISDOM OF PROVERBS

1. heart
2. guard
3. sharpens
4. sword
5. pride
6. summer
7. wisdom
8. medicine
9. wrath
10. paths straight
11. loves
12. commands

GOSPEL GOODNESS MATCHING GAME

1. Mark
2. Matthew
3. John
4. Luke
5. John
6. Mark
7. Matthew
8. Matthew
9. John
10. Luke
11. Mark
12. Mark
13. Matthew
14. John
15. Luke
16. Luke

JESUS'S FAMILY HISTORY

1. Adam
2. Noah
3. Abraham
4. Jacob
5. Judah
6. David
7. Solomon
8. Josiah
9. Joseph
10. Mary
11. Rahab
12. Enoch
13. Methuselah

WHICH EMPIRE DO THESE BELONG TO?

1. Persia
2. Persia
3. Greece
4. Rome
5. Babylon
6. Greece
7. Rome
8. Babylon
9. Babylon
10. Greece
11. Rome
12. Babylon
13. Persia
14. Greece
15. Persia

PROPHESY MATCHING

1. Luke 1:32
2. Matthew 2:1
3. Matthew 1:22-23
4. Matthew 13:34-35
5. Matthew 21:1-11
6. John 13:18
7. John 20:25-27
8. John 19:33-36
9. Mark 16:5-6
10. Acts 1:9-11

JESUS: THE GOD-MAN

HUMANITY

He breathed air

He was hungry and thirsty

He wasn't glamorous or notable in appearance

He was tired

He cried

He grew from a baby to an adult

He bled and died

DIVINITY

He is all-powerful

He is sovereign

He is eternal, living before He became a human

He is able to forgive sins

He received worship from his followers

He is present everywhere

He is all-knowing

WHERE ON EARTH DID IT ALL BEGIN?

1. galaxy
2. moon
3. dust
4. eclipse
5. star
6. element
7. Sabbath
8. light-year
9. constellation
10. asteroid
11. Milky Way
12. eternal
13. planet
14. black hole
15. solar system

Hidden Message: God Created It All

4 GOSPELS, 18 QUESTIONS, ALL GOOD NEWS

1. John
2. longest
3. New Testament
4. four
5. apostles
6. Messiah
7. Good News
8. Christ
9. shortest
10. Levi
11. evangelist
12. doctor
13. Son
14. Old Testament
15. synoptic
16. tax collector
17. Matthew
18. Jesus

Hidden Message: Jesus is the Good News

1. third
2. resurrection
3. spear
4. Golgotha
5. God
6. Son
7. soldiers
8. donkey
9. Judas
10. Last Supper
11. Palm Sunday
12. Pilate
13. it is finished
14. Jesus
15. two
16. mankind
17. cross
18. crown of thorns
19. Simon

ROYALLY FUN POP QUIZ

1. D — Samuel
2. C — sling
3. B — 2.2 trillion dollars
4. A — 7 years old
5. A — Judah's greatest king
6. A — grandson
7. B — worst
8. C — longest-reigning

EPIC BIBLE TRIVIA

PEOPLE IN THE BIBLE

1. Balaam
2. Methuselah, 969 years
3. Sarah
4. Isaac, "he laughs"
5. Elijah
6. Paul
7. Deborah
8. Shadrach, Meshach, and Abednego

THE BIBLE

9. 66
10. Hebrew
11. 2 Samuel
12. Psalms
13. Psalms 119, 176
14. 3 John (219 words)
15. Luke
16. Jude

PLACES IN THE BIBLE

17. Nineveh
18. Bethlehem, Micah
19. Egypt
20. on the road to Damascus
21. Jericho
22. Mount Sinai
23. the mountains of Ararat
24. the Red Sea

POTPOURRI

25. animals and people
26. frogs
27. the Ten Commandments, a pot of manna, and Aaron's staff
28. a coin
29. a donkey
30. a lyre
31. gold, frankincense, and myrrh
32. 12, Matthew

Did you solve the maze to discover my favorite breakfast food? It's WAFFLES!

JESUS'S FAMILY TREE

```
E S U S T A M A R R I S T
E N O C H H J O S E P H S
E S O M R U T H O H N O O
F J J A E G O D B O T A L
L O E E H T H E A B S B O
E S H O N B H N T O S R M
V I O O A O F U H A E A O
I A I H J M S S S M T H N
I H A A E D J H H E H A N
S R C A S A A E E M L M M
A N H D S V C M B T A A H
A E I S E I O O A N D R H
C O N F D D B A V A I D Y
```

Hidden message: Jesus is the Son of God, the Son of Man, and the Son of David!

LIGHT AND DARK

```
O N M U R T C E P S D F R
B O R A D I O R I N O A A
M I C R O W A V E O E H I
I T D O O G H B L Y I G N
N C S L I T L I T D X G B
V E H T U I S H D I R Y O
I T N R N H G E E T A R W
S O T D N I N R R R Y O O
I R T E L O I V A R T L U
B P S D A R K M R T S O E
L S L I V E M T F U S C F
E T E R N A L H N E D A I
R K T H G I L N I E S S L
```

Secret Message: God brings light into the darkness!

WHAT'S THE DEAL WITH THE TABERNACLE?

```
W H G B F L S Q E P O D Y V E
M P C A H O T C L R E N K E E
K E R R L A I N P C R A D I Q
N K L O U F D Z M O I T W L T
X E M A I H S G E M F S E Y H
X O D R S N C A T M T P L N U
N O C E O U U L V A Y M L M T
J A P R V Y R T B N Q A I A I
S Q A H O L Y E D D F L N N O
H A L T A R R M J M B K G N A
T N E M E N O T A E K R A A T
V V U D A S R K H N W D E E V
C C L C E P Y V S T E L B A T
C O L S H Y V J A S P Q V C D
G E C O V E N A N T E K O M S
```

WORDS OF PSALMS

```
N Z V I Z W J G D C H T R A E
E E S V L N D H D S K M X B E
G V V F E A R S E R U D N E M
C H I L D R E N W A U L J F A
I S E G Y L D I Z Q R E P E N
A K G D O N C L D U X T V A G
Y N N A M K J R H P E O P L E
X A X K E D O G O R L C G B P
H H D D K L T K Q N X N E T R
S T E A D F A S T P I I A V A
O R E V E R O F R S K E C K I
U K Y O E V I L C B R Z Y M S
L Q Z S U O E H T G I R D P E
S L W T H G I R X K V Z U G X
X A Z T W I V F N L O O Q L H
```

	Ahab	Solomon	Jehoiachin	Josiah
1010 BC		✓		
870 BC	✓			
640 BC				✓
595 BC			✓	
Amon				✓
David		✓		
Jehoiakim			✓	
Omri	✓			
Elijah	✓			
Habakkuk				✓
Jeremiah			✓	
Nathan		✓		

	Giraffe	Pig	Snake	Dove
Roof Deck				✓
Upper Deck	✓			
Middle Deck		✓		
Lower Deck			✓	
Noah			✓	
Shem	✓			
Ham				✓
Japheth		✓		
Day 10		✓		
Day 20	✓			
Day 30			✓	
Day 40				✓

BEARD ME

RAINBOWS ARE A-MAZE-ING

WISE MAN MAZE

FISHY MONEY

ESCAPE FROM EGYPT

ESTHER
The Brave Queen

GOLIATH
The Warrior Giant

JOSEPH
The Shepherd Dreamer

CAIN
The First Murderer

SPOT **LIGHT**

125

NATIVITY SPOT THE DIFFERENCES

SEA AND SKY—SPOT WHAT DOESN'T BELONG!

WILL THEY ALL FIT?

EASY

HARD

DID **DONKEY** DISAPPEAR?

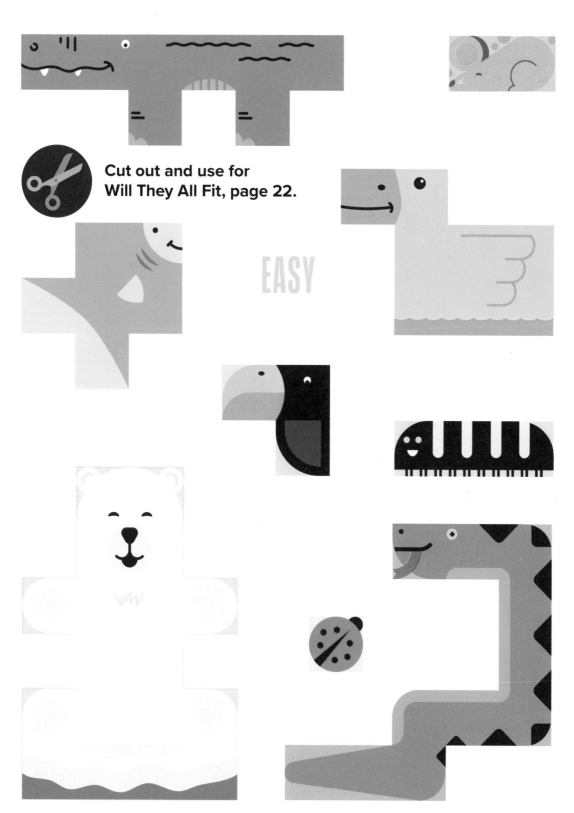

Cut out and use for
Will They All Fit, page 22.

EASY

HARD

Page
23

Cut out and use for the Angelcopter, page 117.

Don't forget to color it in and add more fun details!